DONNA BRYSON

It's a
Black
White
thing

Tafelberg

Tafelberg
An imprint of NB Publishers,
a division of Media24 Boeke (Pty) Ltd
40 Heerengracht, Cape Town
www.tafelberg.com

© Donna Bryson (2014)
Cover photo © Gallo Images

Cover design: Michelle Staples
Book design: Nazli Jacobs
Editing: Mark Ronan
Proofreading: Nicola Rijsdijk

Printed and bound by Paarl Media Paarl,
Jan van Riebeeck Drive, Paarl, South Africa
First edition, first impression 2014
ISBN: 978-0-624-06518-0
Epub: 978-0-624-06519-7
Mobi: 978-0-624-06520-3

— To my family —

Sing a song full of the faith
that the dark past has taught us,
Sing a song full of the hope
that the present has brought us.

From the poem
'Lift Ev'ry Voice and Sing' by
James Weldon Johnson (1871–1938)

Contents

Prologue

'Sjambok' is one of those Afrikaans words that non-Afrikaner South Africans of all languages have imported. Seemingly simply because it sounds so much like what it is: blunt and violent. No South African would call it a mere whip.

Picture a stocky, ruddy man in khaki shorts wielding a sjambok, preferably made from the hide of some large, tough wild animal. This is the stereotypical image people have of a farmer from the Free State, the heartland province as locked in South Africans' imaginations as Alabama or Mississippi are in Americans'.

Stereotypes can be understood as one of the ways we tell stories. They can be a place to start, but go beyond the stereotype and you find a fuller, richer story.

Once, dining alone in a restaurant in Bloemfontein, I was invited to join a group of young professional South Africans, all originally from elsewhere in the country. Here I was, a black American journalist, sitting at a table with black South Africans, surrounded by tables filled with other black South Africans at the back of the restaurant. The white diners were all seated at the front.

I asked whether my dining companions had noticed the restaurant segregation, something I had not experienced elsewhere in South Africa, even in the tense 1990s, when I had visited towns large and small across the country. My companions had noticed, and said it was common in restaurants in Bloemfontein. As transplants from other South African provinces, they had heard that some of their white fellow citizens in the Free State had a reputation for brutal, intractable racism. They said they were afraid to protest when a restaurant host invariably led them to the back.

At the turn of the century, I had met Mothusi Lepheane, an advocate raised in the Eastern Cape who had worked in Johannesburg before moving to Bloemfontein to head the provincial office of the South African Human Rights Commission. He told me: 'You find that this part of the country, some parts of it are 20 years back. There are still places here where racists don't even know they are racist. It's just the way they were raised.'

Many South Africans from other provinces think of racism in the Free State as something particularly marked compared to elsewhere, as if bred into the DNA of the farmers who have for generations sent their sons and daughters to the province's premier university to turn them into doctors and lawyers and Dutch Reformed Church *dominees*.

Stereotypes, like lies, are best kept simple. The complicated truth of the province of the Free State, its university and their histories is that they are a microcosm, not an exception. The truth of this one place holds lessons for many other places, across South Africa and beyond.

New South Africans are bringing all their identities to the project of creating a national identity right here in the university in Bloemfontein. Some combine myriad identities in one family history. The complex, brilliant, kaleidoscope that is South Africa can be found on the campus of the University of the Free State (UFS). Its students are not stereotypes, but individuals striving to build a community.

The Free State's sleepy, provincial university found itself at the centre of an international uproar over a video some of its white students made in 2007 to announce their opposition to racial integration in their hall of residence. The video became public, on the Internet, in early 2008. The students' video showing them humiliating the black women who cleaned their dormitories was viewed worldwide on YouTube and discussed on Facebook, making UFS an international symbol of the persistence of racism in South Africa. The idea that South Africans studying at the university more than a decade after apartheid's end would go to great lengths to record such sentiments was perhaps as shocking as the video's images of casual racism.

I experienced these events as a journalist with some first-hand historical perspective. I had reported from South Africa for the news agency Associated Press from 1993 to 1996, a heady time of great optimism. Then, after assignments in Asia, the Middle East and Europe, I returned to Johannesburg as Associated Press chief of bureau in 2008, finding South Africans less euphoric, but still hopeful. I had arrived in time to cover the aftermath of the video scandal.

This book, partly a story of how and why we tell stories, was a chance for me to explore what happened after other journalists had turned their attentions and their cameras away from Bloemfontein, and left the South Africans there alone to determine how to understand their past and use it to tell their own future. Writing this book was an opportunity for me to return to a place I thought I knew. I had, after all, visited Bloemfontein and UFS several times as a reporter before embarking on the book. It meant revisiting a subject, race relations, that is often discussed in easy clichés. As a reporter, my job is to cross lines of race, gender and experience to tell others' stories. But reporters can grow complacent, imagining that listening is the same as engaging. Embarking on a book forced me to dig deeper in a way that will have a lasting effect on my journalism. I had the privilege of engaging in many long talks with people who care deeply about their university and their country, and who believe change is a challenge to which they are equal. I emerged with a deeper understanding of the values and hopes all humans share. I also came away with a renewed commitment to making the simple point, again and again, that we do share a common humanity, and that we have to guard always against backsliding into suspicion, fear or stereotypes.

Racism and the frighteningly wide gap between poor black people and even middle-class white people don't make the Free State exceptional. No corner of South Africa has escaped the burden of apartheid's legacy, just as no corner of the United States of America can claim to be free of my homeland's racial horrors. Yet, in the context of race relations, few places are watched as closely as this province and its university as they confront the meaning of their history. Some here bristle, saying they are being singled out by those more interested in congratulating themselves for being less racist than in genuinely exploring how to end racism.

What I have seen on my many visits to the university is that people from the Free State choose to embrace this sort of scrutiny and their history as inspiration. If they are seen as exceptionally responsible for the horrors of the past, they can be equally exceptionally imaginative in finding solutions for the future. That sense of the possibility of reinvention, that determination to turn a history of hate and racism into fuel to empower those committed to change, are perhaps nowhere so apparent as on the sprawling, tree-shaded campus of UFS.

'Sjambok' is and isn't an Afrikaans word. Its truth is complicated. It comes from the Malay word for a large whip, *cambok*; it is a word shared by – or perhaps snatched from – people Europeans brought as slaves and exiles from Asia to the tip of Africa. It was in Africa that Afrikaners forged their culture and language, now one of South Africa's 11 official languages. With its Dutch foundations and smatterings of Portuguese, Malay and African languages, including that of the indigenous Khoi people, Afrikaans is a linguistic atlas of South African history.

South Africans are masters of the alchemy of borrowing and adapting. Today the Free State needs those transformative skills more than ever.

1. Songs of change

t started with singing that night in 1996. Billyboy Ramahlele feared it would end in a campus race war.

Ramahlele was new on the job – the first black man to head a hall of residence at what was then called the University of the Orange Free State. As head of the Kiepersol residence, he was a university-appointed father figure for the black students who had just begun to arrive in large numbers.

Those who lived on the campus (and for some, it was because they could not afford to live elsewhere) were housed in halls of residence, informally referred to as 'reses'. These were more than just places to live: the reses have historically had great influence over the social, political and intellectual life of the entire student body at the university.

At this university, students apply to res committees for acceptance, often seeking places at the halls where their parents, or even their grandparents, lived and were moulded. The reses have age-old traditions – songs, mottos, secret rites and origin stories – almost a religious ritualism that is not out of place in the pious Free State. And in the past there were initiation rites meant to break down newcomers to the res in preparation for rebuilding them according to the values and expectations of their new community.

Residences have proudly borne names honouring figures like H. F. Verwoerd, the prime minister assassinated in 1966, who, during his eight years in power, oversaw the establishment of a South African republic, long an Afrikaner dream. Many black South Africans revile him as the prime architect of apartheid. Another res was named after Christiaan de Wet, the general who led Boer guerrilla fighters against the British in the 1899–1902 Anglo-Boer War. Historian Thomas Pakenham says that De Wet's force 'was not a majestic fighting machine, like a British column. It was a fighting animal, all muscle and bone'.[1]

Resourcefulness, independence, resilience – Afrikaners prize these qualities, which they believe helped them maintain their community against threats from powerful opponents in the past. And they can take a perverse pride in others' depiction of them as narrow-minded isolationists. Afrikaner parents, Ramahlele says, would send their sons and daughters to the college at Bloemfontein from the province's small towns and isolated farms, telling them to apply to this res or that res because it inculcated the values that they wanted their children to acquire.

'Historically,' he says, 'residences were an extension of other institutions that were shaping an Afrikaner identity. There was government, there was the church, there was the education system – and universities were part of that: they were extensions for shaping what an Afrikaner is. The reason white students didn't want black students living with them was, according to them, because they did not want their culture to be erased.'

Ramahlele was an ANC activist who, since the 1980s, had

been pressing the university to open its doors to black students despite the prevailing apartheid laws. By the time he was appointed to the university staff in 1995 and took up his residence duties in 1996, apartheid was finally defunct, leaving some Afrikaners all the more fiercely determined to hang on to some semblance of power, like the outposts provided by the student halls of residence.

Ramahlele lived through and was a key player in a history that I, a foreign reporter who arrived in South Africa during apartheid's waning days, had missed. He shared his history generously and vividly with me, helping me in my understanding of where South Africa has come from, and in my imagining of where it may be headed.

South Africa had seen its first all-race election in 1994, and Nelson Mandela had stood, tall and sombre, on the steps of Pretoria's red sandstone Union Buildings, long a symbol of white racist rule, to take the oath of office as the country's first black president.

'Our daily deeds as ordinary South Africans must produce an actual South African reality that will reinforce humanity's belief in justice, strengthen its confidence in the nobility of the human soul and sustain our hopes for a glorious life for all,' Mandela told the nation in his 10 May 1994 inaugural address.[2]

At that point I was a young American reporter working on my first assignment in South Africa for the Associated Press. I had arrived in 1993, just on the eve of democracy, and would leave in 1996 to work in India, Egypt and the UK before returning for a second stint in South Africa from 2008 to 2012. In 1994 I had watched Mandela's inauguration on television with a family in Soweto, one of the townships to which Johannesburg's black maids, gardeners and other workers were removed during apartheid. The family had welcomed me into their home to report on what it meant for black South Africans to see Mandela become president.

I watched them raise their fists in the air as the first strains of the national anthem were played, sounding tinny from the speakers of a small TV set. They saw that Mandela, a tiny figure on the screen, had his hand over his heart. One by one, members of his audience in Soweto lowered their fists, opened their hands and placed them over their hearts. Mandela, South Africa's master alchemist, was transforming a gesture of defiance into one of hope that a new nation was being forged which would command the loyalty of and be welcoming to all who lived there.

For black students at UFS in the mid-1990s, however, that welcome was cold. Many struggled financially and academically. Protesting students, who were demanding that the university write off their debts and offer more classroom support, toyi-toyied on the campus. Most white students had probably only been dimly aware of toyi-toying when the TV news brought anti-apartheid demonstrations into their living rooms.

Black and white students also clashed over seemingly petty issues, like whether to watch soccer or rugby on the res television. South African sports fans are largely divided along race lines, with black fans following soccer, and white fans choosing gby. They may feel it's natural for sport to be racialised, failing to realise the divide is rooted in history and stereotype, and is not something organic to the playing field.

Initiation rituals also rankled. In some reses, first-year students were expected to sit on the floor during house meetings, leaving the chairs to senior students. Initiation rites also included subjecting new students to all-night harangues, or forcing them to run errands for senior students.

Ramahlele was in his 30s when he arrived on campus in January 1996. He met black students who were his age, or older. Some had put in extra years of studying to prepare themselves for university after having undergone the inferior education to which apartheid subjected black people. Others had completed the traditional initiation rites of their ethnic groups, and expected to be treated as men. There were students who were husbands and fathers. Some had taken longer to finish high school because they had been involved in the struggle, and had spent time in jail because of their political activism. Former ANC guerrillas were among the students. And yet, Ramahlele says, here were young white students speaking to them as if they were labourers on their fathers' farms.

'In African culture, you respect your elders. And here's a young Afrikaner boy telling you to sit on the floor,' Ramahlele says. Some of those white students had been conscripted into the apartheid government's army. Says Ramahlele:

You had black people, males in particular, who were fresh from the struggle, fresh from prison, fresh from detention, fresh from military training. And they're thrown into the same residential area with whiteys. You also had Afrikaans boys who came from military conscription, who had been trained that a black man was an enemy. Trained also in other aspects of racism against black people. And here, for the first time, they meet at the University of the Free State.

Ramahlele explains that the university's management team were not trained for these realities. 'At that stage, every Afrikaner male had done military service,' he says, referring to university managers who would have come of age before national service was abolished in 1992. 'So, you had an ideological and a political conflict. The whole system of Afrikaner leadership was trained to see a black man with a different eye. And now you had black students who were resisting being seen in that way.'

Ramahlele says black students were too much of a minority to be elected to places on the committees that set the rules in the halls of residence. They felt vulnerable as the minority, he says, especially when the confrontations got physical.

The reses on one side of the campus became predominantly black. That area, Ramahlele says, was dubbed the 'Bantustan', an ironic reference to the nominally segregated black homelands established during apartheid. The white part of campus, Ramahlele says, was known as the Volkstaat.

Ramahlele's res, Kiepersol, was integrated when he arrived

but the white students left, and the black students who remained were particularly politicised. Some may have been drawn by the presence of Ramahlele, whose anti-apartheid activism was well known.

Ramahlele sees himself as a 'Christian activist'. He has a degree in theology. 'For me,' he says, 'Christianity does not necessarily mean pacifism. There are certain things that, if you want to destroy them, you don't have to be violent, but you have to be physical. Christ did that.'

One can imagine that Ramahlele, a vigorous man with close-cropped hair, is as comfortable in the pulpit at the Bloemfontein church where he preaches as he is behind his UFS desk, where he is still a manager today. Ramahlele believes universities should teach universal, not narrow, group values and that university halls of residence should be places where people can learn to live with one another. But he recognises that, even now, this is a point of contention in universities across the world.

Many of the black students at Kiepersol were leading figures in student organisations affiliated with the ANC and other, more radical black groups. Ramahlele's charges recruited more black students, offering them protection from the assaults and other abuse they faced in the predominantly white reses. Kiepersol was a senior residence, meaning that everyone who lived there had already spent at least a year at the university. For black students, that first year was very likely to be a tough one.

Ramahlele says that Kiepersol had disaffected black students who challenged the system:

I inherited a res which was very angry at the system, very angry at the white people. I inherited students who were once abused within the system. And, as a result, Kiepersol became almost a political institution, for protecting the rights of blacks on campus. And I had to head that. But I'm also a manager in a white system. I had to say, 'There's anger, understandably so. But the expression of this anger needs to be channelled in a responsible way.'

'Blackness was being affirmed and respected under my leadership,' Ramahlele says, proud that Kiepersol residents were among the first blacks to gain places in student-union leadership positions.

But the future looked uncertain that night of the singing. Ramahlele was at home in the apartment attached to his res, where he lived with his wife. He heard the sound of protest songs dating from the anti-apartheid struggle getting louder outside. 'I was worried because I had never heard so many students singing at that time of night,' he says, recalling that it was around 8 o'clock in the evening. He went outside the res to find students armed with bats. He approached them to find out what was going on and they told him they were very angry. Some black students had been assaulted and abused in a residence called D. F. Malherbe. The Kiepersol students were going to rescue them.

Ramahlele tried to dissuade them, telling them the white students outnumbered them and that they were likely to be better armed. Nevertheless, they set out anyway, about 140 of them, some with guns, toward the Volkstaat res. Ramahlele called the director of student housing, and told him he thought a war was going to break out. Then he followed his Kiepersol men.

The white students, meanwhile, had heard trouble was coming. 'The white students were also being mobilised and organised. They had their bats, and I saw they also had guns,' Ramahlele remembers.

The white students had called in reinforcements who lived off campus, and they began arriving in their cars. Few black students could afford cars.

The black students toyi-toyied; the white students sang 'Die Stem'. The national anthem of the apartheid government had, with the dawn of democracy, been combined with a hymn of the anti-apartheid movement, 'Nkosi Sikelel'iAfrika', in what was meant to be the uniting theme of a new South Africa. The Xhosa, Zulu and Sotho lyrics of 'Nkosi Sikelel'iAfrika' call for divine help in banishing wars and strife. 'Die Stem' proudly extolls the beauties of the country.

There was no such harmony on campus that night in 1996. Ramahlele, however, was able to persuade the black students to retreat when they saw the growing force of white students. As the black students ran back to Kiepersol, they smashed the windows of parked cars, which to them symbolised white privilege and arrogance. The white students followed them. Hundreds, if not thousands, surrounded the black students, who had now reached the safety of their res. The white students threw stones, breaking every window in the building. The police arrived, as did higher-ranking campus officials. White officials pleaded with the students outside; Ramahlele kept talking to the students inside, and kept in touch with his colleagues by phone. Around midnight, the white students were persuaded to return to their reses.

Among the senior officials who rushed to the campus to help Ramahlele was Benito Khotseng. In 1993 Khotseng had become one of the university's first black senior managers. Years later he would offer me further insight into this piece of history and was, like Ramahlele, willing to relive the turmoil of the past. The two also display a remarkable resilience that I see as the real story, a theme that comes up again and again in the stories of South Africans.

Early on, Khotseng's job had entailed recruiting students. He also took on the role of finding scholarships for black students, and creating special classes to ensure that students who had had the inferior education afforded them during apartheid could keep up academically at a formerly white university. And although not a formal part of his job description, Khotseng's duties, out of necessity, came to include trying to keep racial confrontations from flaring into violence.

Another confrontation in 1997 nearly spun out of control at Karee, a residence that had suddenly seen its proportion of blacks rise from zero to 30 per cent. White students at Karee surreptitiously added a laxative to the sandwiches served to the students at afternoon tea. The white students made sure black students got the tainted food, saying they resented the newcomers helping themselves to what they saw as unfair portions. The laxative had a powerful effect: several badly dehydrated students had to be hospitalised.

The next day, retaliation came for the laxative stunt. Two firebombs were thrown at guards at the university's front gates. Dozens of black students descended on a central hall where exams were being administered. The white students fled, leaving their black counterparts toyi-toying outside the hall. More white students began heading to the hall from residences then notorious for their militant racism – Reitz, J. B. M. Hertzog, Verwoerd.

While a white senior member of university management, Vice-Rector Teuns Verschoor, pleaded with the white students to return to their residences, Khotseng did the same with the black ones. Eventually, the two sides were separated. 'Later on, I asked Teuns, "What do you think happened?",' Khotseng recalls, sitting in the dining room of his home on the edge of campus. His face is unlined, but thick-lensed bifocals hint at his years. Verschoor and Khotseng came to the conclusion that, for all the meticulous planning to bring more black students to the university, including installing Ramahlele as a res head, they had not given enough time to prepare black and white students to study and live together.

It's not that Khotseng and other university officials did not understand there was a challenge to be overcome. Ramahlele would not have been hired as a res head had they not. And Khotseng had been a frequent visitor to black, white and integrated residences. He'd spoken to students about what to expect and what was expected of them. Students regularly came to his office with questions. He had taken to spending weekends on campus, mentoring and advising students. But, in the end, Khotseng came to believe he should have done more, and done it more systematically.

'In a way, I realised we let change take place very fast, without facilitating it,' he says. 'We encouraged black students to come to campus. But the effort that we put in to convince white students to accept black students as their equals was very little. Many of the Afrikaans students who came to the university were from farms,' he says, explaining that these students' exposure to black South Africans had been hitherto limited to the farm labourers on their families' estates. When they got to the university, they had to accept black students as their equals. 'We did very little to assist them to change. We should have done a lot more homework. We should really have worked on them,' he says.

Khotseng had fastidiously prepared for his role at UFS. His first experience of the university was in the 1980s. The former high-school teacher had risen to become an administrator in the education department of the government of Qwaqwa, the impoverished homeland that the apartheid government had set up for the Free State's Sotho-speakers.

In a tactic that amounted to a subtle undermining of a system meant to smother black people's aspirations, Khotseng sought help from researchers at what was then the University of the

Orange Free State. He wanted advice on planning budgets and curricula. His aim, he said, was to improve education for blacks. And white people helped him.

'In order to see the success of apartheid, I guess, they were bound, in a way, to support us in separate development,' he says. Not that his welcome was warm. As he visited the library and offices of the university, he found himself challenged by white students and staff who seemed incapable of addressing him in a normal tone of voice. 'There used to be a lot of anti-black people,' he says. 'I was never really accepted.'

This was just a few years after the rector of the university had severely reprimanded, according to the university's official history, the captain of the student chess team for taking part in a chess tournament at another university where non-white (in this case, Chinese) players had been welcomed.[3]

'I was one of the first black people to come to campus as a researcher and visit the library,' Khotseng says. 'People used to shout at me. They would be howling at me: "What do you want? What are you doing here?" And I would say, "I'm here doing research."'

In the early 1990s, Sotho-speakers began to champion the idea of a 'university for *ourselves*', as Khotseng puts it, drawing out the last word for emphasis. He was among those who advocated a partnership with UFS. He explained how he had learnt to work with Afrikaners while doing research there in the 1980s. Many Sotho-speakers also spoke Afrikaans, and the Qwaqwa administration was already working closely with Orange

Free State bureaucrats, many of whom had trained at what would become UFS. 'I worked with them and understood them and how they worked,' Khotseng says, referring to Afrikaners.

Khotseng also portrays this proposal to UFS as a tactic in the fight against the system that had established universities based on the race of their students. 'People wanted to defeat apartheid,' he says. His colleagues 'wanted to indicate to the government that there should be but one university. They realised it would not be possible to have more than one university in the Free State.'

But Qwaqwa's overtures to what it saw as the natural partner for a university for its people were rebuffed. Officials were directed to work instead with the University of the North, an institution established for black people. However, the University of the North was some 700 kilometres from Qwaqwa (in what is now Polokwane) and in a region where blacks were as likely to speak Tsonga or Venda as Sotho. It was poorly funded compared with UFS, as Khotseng knew, as that is where he had completed his master's. As the UFS history relates in matter-of-fact prose, with the entrenchment of apartheid in the 1950s, 'the white government provided white, Afrikaans universities with generous financial support'.[4]

In the early 1990s, a University of the North campus was established in Qwaqwa. Khotseng taught philosophy and education there, and became dean of its education department. In 2003 that Qwaqwa campus became part of UFS.

In the 1990s, ambitions were being realised in South Africa. In December 1989, a prisoner met a president – Nelson Mandela and F. W. de Klerk. On 2 February 1990, De Klerk unbanned Mandela's ANC, and in Paarl nine days later Mandela walked from prison to be greeted by cheering crowds. In 1993, negotiators representing Mandela and De Klerk, and others completed a draft Constitution that opened the way to all-race elections on 27 April 1994.

Bloemfontein, once the capital of an independent Afrikaner republic, now has a Nelson Mandela Drive, winding from a shabby neighbourhood of mechanics' garages and used-furniture shops, past the city hall, and on to a new part of the town, which sports a mall and the gleaming regional offices of large South African corporations. The main gate of UFS is on Nelson Mandela Drive.

As the date neared for South Africa's first free elections, university officials let it be known they wanted a black educator to help put them on the map of a new South Africa.

'I applied with interest,' Khotseng says. 'Here was an opportunity for me to assist the university and assist the Afrikaner to change, and to help us achieve what we wanted – which was to improve education for blacks in the Free State.'

He got the job, but Khotseng wanted to be sure that those who hired him saw him as a member of the team, not an outsider who was simply being tolerated. The language issue was revealing. Sitting at his dining-room table, Khotseng pulls a copy of letter from a file that he sent to the rector in February

1993, in Afrikaans, asking where his new post fell within the university structure. He insisted on a job title and a clear job description that he felt reflected the position he had assumed. The rector responded to the effect that Khotseng was his adviser on special projects – raising funds for scholarships for black students, planning multicultural training to help black and white students and staff learn about one another, and recruiting black students and staff.

That clarified the role, but Khotseng wanted to find out exactly where he fitted into the organisation. 'I challenged them. So the principal had to go to the council. In the end, they said that they would establish my post as deputy vice-rector for student affairs,' Khotseng says of the title he was eventually given. It was a breakthrough for a black academic at any formerly white university in South Africa.

He also asked that his daughter Nthabiseng be enrolled at the university, another step he had to take up with university officials. His daughter's presence made it all the more important that an atmosphere welcoming to black students be created, Khotseng says. More black students would have to be recruited, a task he took on, along with identifying staff members who would be willing to help the new students settle in. And he urged the rector to take steps to train and nurture black academics who could rise in staff positions at the university.

Khotseng came to change a university, but he says he quickly realised he would have to change himself first. He had been a high-school teacher, a university professor and an education bureaucrat in a segregated system. He knew he was no expert in transformation. So Khotseng began to read, exploring studies on the psychology of race and on race in the workplace. He took a six-month management course at Harvard.

He encouraged colleagues to conduct at least some university business in English, but also worked on his Afrikaans. He told them, 'You guys have helped me to learn Afrikaans. We must take this a step further: you must learn Sotho. I must teach you Sotho.'

His colleagues, he says, were excited at the opportunity. He put together a Sotho phrase book for managers, and the Afrikaners who used it almost immediately saw the benefits in terms of better relations with the black cleaners and other support staff they had once taken for granted.

'I had first of all to change my attitudes towards other people in order to be able to change them,' he says. 'I realised I had to get interested in their way of life, and show them things that could get them interested in my way of life.'

Language, then, did not have to be a point of departure. Black and white South Africans share this: they hold their native tongues dear, and that can be an opening to learning to respect one another's languages in a nation that today has 11 official tongues. 'I didn't have any problem speaking Afrikaans,' he says. 'But I insisted they also should speak Sotho.'

Khotseng sought allies, many of them the white women who felt undervalued in tradition-bound, patriarchal Afrikaner society. He championed the promotion of white women to senior positions. Here was a black man able to see the world from the point of view of white women:

> When I came here, women – even though they were white – were in a way discriminated against, left out, in terms of management. I started bringing up the issue of women in management. White women saw me as someone who brought them in. That made it quite easy for me to work with white women on campus. They saw that I was very positive as far as they were concerned, that I felt they needed to be treated as equals and that they needed to be given opportunities.

As he speaks, Khotseng places his hands together under his chin, fingertips lightly touching, as if he were holding a delicate piece of pottery. Khotseng says his experience at UFS taught him that change has to be handled as if it were something fragile. He believes that the unrest in the campus in the mid-1990s resulted from a failure to communicate and monitor. The bridges he had built to women in the university helped his mission because he was able to speak to the women who headed the female residences. He learnt that they had worked to welcome the black students – something the heads of the male residences had not done. The female residences had not experienced the kind of turmoil that the male residences had, he says.

Then, Khotseng explains, university officials, shocked and uncertain, made another mistake: they did not continue to demand that students integrate their reses.

'We should have pushed for it during that period,' he says. 'We should have worked hard to try to encourage it more and more. And we didn't.'

Khotseng shows an adeptness for adaptation I have come to see as quintessentially South African. His own story, with the rebuffs he first experienced in Bloemfontein and the violence he was unable to prevent later, could have been a blueprint for bitterness. But I hear strength in the calm with which he tells his story to me. His is a journey that tempers and teaches.

2. Nation building

A stone obelisk rises from a stubby hill on the outskirts of Bloemfontein: the Women's Monument. At the foot of the stone tower, a bronze sculpture of a woman sits cradling a dying child in her lap. She is watched over by another woman whose flowing hood and gown recall angels' wings. An inscription on the monument reads that it is dedicated to the 26 370 women and children who died in the British concentration camps of the Anglo-Boer War of 1899 to 1902.

The Afrikaners in the two Boer republics, the Orange Free State and the Transvaal, lost their independence in a war that dragged on, with Afrikaner guerrillas resisting a larger foe. The British rounded up the women and children – and their black farmworkers – into camps that have endured as symbols of the cruelty of this war.

Historian Thomas Pakenham writes of the scorched-earth campaign that the large British Army resorted to out of frustration at being unable to swiftly crush the small, mobile, resourceful Boer commando units. It started on a small scale, with orders to burn a few farms, but the Boers were determined to hold on to their independence. Pakenham refers to this dogged determination in his exhaustive history of the war:[5] 'Husbands and sons in the hills fighting. Homes in the valley blazing. And the women sitting there watching, with the same patience, the same absolute confidence in ultimate victory, as the guerrillas.'

Pakenham explains how some British officers were both disturbed and impressed by the Boers' resistance: 'They had never seen anything before quite like this "big, primitive" kind of patriotism. But most British officers were all for farm burning. They thought that Sister Boer was as stubborn and stupid, to put it no worse, as Brother Boer himself.'[6]

The farm burnings, essentially attacks on the civilian population to keep them from helping the enemy, were stepped up in late 1900. But Britain saw itself as too civilised to allow the refugees it had created to wander the veld homeless and starving, so a plan was devised to corral them into camps. Perhaps because it was wartime, perhaps because no one had paused to consider the immense scale of the task they were embarking on, or perhaps because the British harboured contempt for the women and children of their enemy, the camps were woefully inadequate.

British welfare campaigner Emily Hobhouse, the daughter of an Anglican clergyman and niece of anti-war politician Lord Hobhouse, went to South Africa to visit the camps for herself in 1900. Her report, delivered to members of the British Parliament, and her lobbying caused a storm in Britain – and beyond. Hobhouse is remembered in South Africa for speaking out about the camps and returning after the war to start education and economic-development projects for Afrikaner women – the wives and daughters of the enemy. After her death in 1926, her ashes were brought to Bloemfontein to be installed in a niche in the Women's Monument – a memorial to those who had died in the camps. Her remains rest there, an Englishwoman remembered among Afrikaners with loving respect.

The reality of that grave speaks to a feat of imagination, of invention, on both sides. Hobhouse, after whom a UFS women's hostel is named, was able to put herself in the place of the suffering women and children she found a world away from her own privileged English home. And Afrikaners were able to see her as a sister and a mother, not as a speaker of an enemy tongue, an aloof colonialist offering charity.

Among the largest of the Boer War camps was the one at Bloemfontein, which fell to Britain in 1900, two years before the Boer generals would finally surrender.

Defeated and still heartsore, Afrikaners unveiled the Women's Monument in 1913. And, bitterly determined to rise again, Boer War veterans were among the first students of the faculty founded in 1904 that would eventually become the University of the Free State.

That institution had its roots in a seminary known as Grey College, which had opened in Bloemfontein in 1856. It was named after George Grey, a governor of Britain's Cape Colony, who had secured a grant from Britain to start a Dutch Reformed school for what was then the Republic of the Orange Free State. Grey's school was perhaps a reconciliatory gesture on the part of the British authorities towards the men and women who, since the 1830s, had trekked out of the Cape to form their own republic.

Grey College offered a limited number of courses and students had to travel to Cape Town, in the opposite direction of their ancestors' trek, to take examinations and classes for higher degrees. They could study in English in Cape Town or travel to the Netherlands to study in Dutch. In 1904, when six students registered for bachelor studies in Bloemfontein, government funds were made available for the first university building. Thus Grey University College was born. The first students were all white men; women enrolled a few years later.

The first graduation was in 1905. More buildings were added, and its name was changed in 1935 to University College of the Orange Free State. The university's nickname among students, which lives on today, is 'Kovsies' – derived from the Afrikaans name Kollege van die Oranje-Vrystaat. The institution became the University of the Orange Free State in 1950 and the University of the Free State in 2001.

The Afrikaners craved and established an independent university, though it would take decades to create a curriculum in Afrikaans and offer instruction in Afrikaans, as opposed to English or Dutch.

The university's official history quotes the revered Afrikaner nationalist F. W. Reitz (after whom the student hall of residence made infamous by the so-called Reitz video is named – see Chapter 3): in 1894 Reitz had argued that Afrikaners needed a university of their own 'in the interest of our independence, and in order to preserve nationality'.[7] The suffering and defeat in war only served to deepen these desires. A lawyer who had served both Afrikaner republics before they fell to Britain, Reitz was president of the Free State and wartime foreign secretary of the neighbouring Transvaal.

In many respects, the university owes its origins more to the message symbolised by that stone tower in the hills than any aspirations to being an ivory tower: it was an ideological and nation-building, or rebuilding, project in which a particular community invested its hopes for the future. The Afrikaners were setting out to reinvent themselves as victors.

About a decade after the peace treaty that had ended the Boer War, some of the most prominent Boer generals raised a rebellion against the Union government's decision to support Britain in World War I. Brother fought against brother, and once-revered Boer generals were sentenced to jail, the university history recalls, adding that the internecine split extended to the campus. Some students sided with the South African government led by Prime Minister Louis Botha and J. C. Smuts, both Afrikaner heroes of the Boer War; some followed another war hero, Christiaan de Wet, into insurrection.[8] Scores of rebels and loyalist fighters were killed in the short-lived uprising. De Wet, after whom a UFS hostel is named, was later convicted of high treason, but his fine was paid by supporters and he served only six months of his six-year prison sentence.[9] Although the university history is not explicit on the subject, many students who had joined the rebels no doubt eventually returned to their studies. I wonder how many drew, from the leniency shown De

Wet and his largely undiminished reputation, the lesson that Afrikaner nationalism would and should rise again.

Initiation traditions devised by students, which would have a profound influence on the personality of the university for many years to come, began to emerge around the same time. A blurry 1912 photo shows four men in costumes that make them resemble extras from a movie whose art director has an uncertain grasp of Roman history. According to the caption, they are the Torture Committee, charged with 'welcoming' new students to the university.[10]

The caption describes the futures of the young men pictured: they would become doctors and professors. One was C. R. Swart, who would become a South African president. They were influential men from respected families, who would go on to hold their own respected positions in the Afrikaner community. The university history goes on to describe the initiation ceremonies presided over by secretive societies led by these and other young men and women. The societies were based at the student halls of residence, which would develop into social and political centres of the campus, and play a crucial, and sometimes divisive, role in later attempts to integrate the university.

What did these ceremonies entail? Newcomers were spanked, denied sleep, forced to run gauntlets in which they were slapped with wet towels. They polished the shoes of older students, and collected their laundry and post. They were made distinguishable so that any older student knew who to harass – the young men in jackets turned inside out with their trouser legs rolled up, the young women in dresses worn back to front, or their hair conspicuously braided.

Since the 1920s, university officials have repeatedly tried to ban, or at least limit, the initiation abuse – even through semantic efforts (the name 'Torture Committee' was compulsorily changed to 'Welcoming Committee' in 1937). But, despite these efforts, students were determined to persist, confident they were contributing in their own way to the goals of their university and their community. The university history quotes a letter that students wrote to the local newspaper soon after the university's founding:

> We wish, through initiation, simply to show the newcomer that ... he knows nothing and is nothing. His ego must be broken down slightly so that his future moral and intellectual development can take place from a healthy base. Our initiation is directed at the psychological, not the physical, side of the student. Indeed, to be able to build securely, we want first of all to break down those aspects that are wrong.[11]

An earnest, if unsophisticated, rendering of the belief – and one that is certainly not unique among Afrikaners – that suffering builds men and societies, that defeat strengthens. Just a few generations after those university students outlined their strategy, young South African men would encounter something similar when they were drafted into the apartheid government's army, to fight in the townships that were home to fellow South Africans who were black, or to fight the Border War against countries where black politicians had taken over from white colonialists. One former conscript, who went AWOL, told the Truth and Reconciliation Commission: 'The aim of basic training ... was not to equip you with battle skills but ... to break you down so that you would blindly follow orders.'[12]

Alchemy does not come without a cost.

A reader dipping into the university history finds the same questions raised again and again, seemingly never to be settled: issues of language, of how much responsibility a student should be given and what manner of leader should be shaped. The students were both subjects of and participants in a continual discussion over identity.

After the Anglo-Boer War, Afrikaners may have chafed at what they saw as English meddling in their relations with black South Africans, and the English may have believed themselves to be more liberal. But in the new Union of South Africa, created after the war, white English victors and white Afrikaner losers alike subjugated black South Africans. The fierce debates then were not over race, but over language.

In 1904, at the founding of what would become the university, the Afrikaner students were taught in English because of the dearth of professors trained to teach them in Afrikaans. Nevertheless, from the start, Afrikaners campaigned for a university they could call their own – one where the medium of instruction would be Afrikaans. The Anglo-Boer War was still fresh in

Afrikaners' minds, as were memories of the British officers who viewed Afrikaners as primitive and stubbornly resistant, and who had brought the war to Afrikaner women and children with their scorched-earth campaign. Having their children taught in the language of this victor was anathema.

In 1918 the National University of South Africa granted its affiliates permission to teach in Afrikaans. In the same year, D. F. Malherbe, a professor at Grey University College and later rector, became the nation's first professor of Afrikaans.[13]

But most courses were still taught in English in Bloemfontein. Afrikaner politicians, journalists and clergy campaigned for Afrikaans at the university, though some Afrikaners opposed abolishing English because they wanted to see South Africa's white communities united.

In the 1930s, Grey University College and other Afrikaans institutions broke away from the National Union of South African Students, which was seen as liberal and English, and allied itself with a new student union that had an unabashedly Afrikaner nationalist agenda, the Afrikaanse Nasionale Studentebond.

It was a time when not only students, but also the larger community of white South Africans were split politically. On the one side there were English- and Afrikaans-speaking South Africans who wanted to remain loyal to the British Crown and who supported Anglo-Boer War general Jan Smuts and his United Party. On the other side were the nationalists who wanted an independent Afrikaner republic. The latter group consisted mostly of Afrikaans-speakers and they supported D. F. Malan's National

Party (NP). Malan became prime minister in 1948 after the NP won the elections. With his coming to power, laws segregating the races and subjugating black South Africans were passed that would eventually develop into apartheid.

On the university campus in 1948, Afrikaner nationalists at last saw their dream realised. English was phased out as a medium of instruction, and the university became a purely Afrikaans institution.

The university history includes excerpts from the work of celebrated Afrikaans historian Karel Schoeman, described as a 'critical outsider' during his years at the university in the 1950s. His words presaged later debates about how to foster excellence at the university:

> With the elevation of 'Afrikaansness' to the one and only criterion, a situation began to develop at the university in the 40s which would affect the whole country in the next decade, namely that appointments were made not because the person concerned was the most suitable, but because he was Afrikaans-speaking – it applied almost without exception to Afrikaans men – and had the 'right' political and religious affiliations. This paved the way for the growth of a considerable phalanx of mediocre, third-rate and generally fatuous officials who, under the guise of 'Afrikaansness' ended up in positions which they never should have held, with a concomitant lowering of standards.[14]

Prime Minister Hendrik Verwoerd came to Bloemfontein in 1963 to receive an honorary degree. Historian and journalist Allister Sparks, in his political history of South Africa, *The Mind of South Africa*, describes Verwoerd as apartheid's Lenin – 'the man who added to [apartheid] conceptually and then sought to put it into practice in its total-separation form'.[15] Verwoerd's name can sound like a curse on the lips of black South Africans.

By the 1970s the Afrikaanse Studentebond had become the main student cultural organisation in the university, and it was becoming more politically assertive and more outspoken about its allegiance to the National Party and apartheid. Roelf Meyer, then a law student at the university, was elected president of the Afrikaanse Studentebond in 1970. Meyer would go on to serve as a National Party Cabinet minister, and, later, as the party's chief negotiator in the talks that led to the end of apartheid.

In the post-apartheid years, as the National Party became increasingly irrelevant, Meyer joined the ANC, which, like the National Party, has its roots in Bloemfontein. Some may see Meyer as an opportunist, even a traitor, for showing that talent for adapting – without which South Africa's transformation to multiracial democracy would have been impossible.

For many South Africans, the 1980s was the decade in which it became clear apartheid was impossible. The government reacted with fear and violence, cracking down on black nationalism, political activism and violence. It was a time when anti-apartheid activists at home and abroad were finding innovative ways to keep up the pressure, and not just politically. The 1980s also saw a major victory in the campaign to isolate South African sportsmen and women because of their country's racist policies: the thwarting of a planned tour of New Zealand by the Springboks.

Sparks describes the violence on the ground:

> By February 1985, for the first time the police found themselves confronted with organised street fighters. In the Crossroads, the 'comrades' made huge shields of corrugated iron which they carried into the street to protect the stone- and petrol-bomb throwers from police shotguns. In Alexandra they dug 'tank traps' – trenches three feet deep – across the rutted roadways to stop the Hippos.[16]

Protests exploded into confrontation, to be followed by dusty mass funerals. Sparks says the 1980s saw the most sustained insurrection hitherto carried out by black South Africans, with the country in 'a virtual state of civil war'.[17] Sparks estimates that the 1984–1987 uprisings led to 3 000 deaths and 30 000 detentions.[18]

In his memoirs, Chester A. Crocker, the US Assistant Secretary of State for African Affairs during that turbulent decade, writes that the 1980s showed that 'the ramshackle system could no longer be defended at an acceptable price. Nor could power be seized at an acceptable price. South Africans on all sides had looked down into the abyss of civil violence – and recoiled in sober shock.'[19]

Yet the reaction in the university to what was happening in

South African society was a passive form of denial. The university history explains that the students were isolated in a predominantly white institution, where 'the reality of the "struggle" outside apparently did not penetrate the thoughts of Kovsies'.[20]

Ignoring that reality was a choice that many white South Africans made. They were surrounded by the turmoil of change, and constantly confronted by ideological and political challenges to how they had defined themselves for generations. Perhaps they hoped that if they decided the challenges were beneath notice, they would indeed prove unimportant. And if a reckoning should one day come, they could at least plead ignorance.

If the students ensconced in the university had decided to ignore the struggle, its momentum had nonetheless reached the Free State despite them. Celebrated liberal Afrikaans writer Antjie Krog writes in her memoirs about a committee that arrived at her door one day in 1987 in Kroonstad to beg her to read her poetry at a rally in Maokeng, Kroonstad's township, lobbying support for Mandela's release from prison. At the time, it was illegal to quote Mandela in South Africa.

She delivered her poem in Afrikaans, and the township crowd turned her refrain into a chant: '*Die vuis sê Mandela! Mandela se Maokeng!*' (The fist says Mandela! Mandela says Maokeng!).[21]

Van Aardt Smit was just 23 in 1982 when he started teaching at what was then the University of the Orange Free State. I tracked him down to find out more about what it was like at the university in those days. Smit had studied at the university, had completed his military service and had hitch-hiked across Europe before becoming a lecturer. Now a UFS business-science professor specialising in entrepreneurship, he remembers the shock of discovery on his tour of Europe.

'You would pick up a newspaper and you would see how the rest of the world felt about South Africa,' he says. 'You would see things you would never see in your own press. It was not nice to see we were probably the most hated country in the world.'

Yet, when he returned to Bloemfontein, he slipped back into a state of unknowing. 'It was almost a little bubble,' he says. 'You didn't realise what was happening.'

He and his friends, he says, held anti-government views that were considered radical for the time, but they did not act on their convictions within the bubble that was Bloemfontein's university.

'We talked a lot. But we didn't do a lot,' he says. 'I don't think we realised to what extent it was ignorance and to what extent it was brainwashing. I think we realised we had a police state. [But] I don't think people sometimes realise how effective the government was in brainwashing the white population.'

Imagine that, only a generation later, in November of 2001, UFS conferred an honorary degree on Mandela. It is a measure of both Mandela's commitment to reconciliation and how far South Africa had travelled that Mandela accepted an honour that the same university had earlier bestowed on Verwoerd.

Mandela gave his acceptance speech in Afrikaans and English: 'Much remains to be done on the road of transformation – and this is true for all sectors of higher education – but the concerted change-seeking efforts of the historically Afrikaans universities should be proudly recognised and acknowledged,' he said. 'What the University of the Free State has done to promote diversity, a multicultural environment and respect and appreciation for all of the traditions and backgrounds of the people of the province and country, has not escaped us. To many, your university represents a model in this regard.'[22]

In 2006, the name of the university's Verwoerd residence was changed to Armentum, Latin for a herd of elephants, the house mascot. In a statement, the then rector Frederick Fourie said the change was 'part of the transformation effort at UFS to make the campus a more inclusive place, where all South Africans can feel at home'.[23]

Verwoerd's National Party, which would fade away soon after apartheid ended, had its beginnings in Bloemfontein, where the Anglo-Boer War general J. B. M. Hertzog (and later prime minister of the Union) formally established the Free State National Party in 1914.

Mandela's ANC, by a coincidence of history and geography, was also born from a meeting that took place in Bloemfontein, in 1912. A year later, the British Parliament would approve the Natives Land Act, barring the black majority from owning land in all but 7.5% of South Africa. The 1912 meeting in Bloemfontein 'was perhaps the first step taken by the peoples of our region, who had been subjugated by three European powers –

Britain, Germany and Portugal – towards creating the institutions needed to defeat colonialism and racial oppression to reclaim the freedom the African people had lost on the battlefield,' the ANC recalls in a historical essay marking the centenary of its founding.[24]

Like the Afrikaners who had regrouped at Bloemfontein to start a university, the black Africans were determined to turn the bitterness of defeat at the hands of colonialism into inspiration for resurrection. Waaihoek, a Bloemfontein district to which black South Africans were restricted during apartheid, is not far from the Women's Monument. Still standing is the church that was the site of the January 1912 founding meeting of the South African Native National Congress, which would become the ANC.

Nearby is the house once owned by Thomas Mapikela, a local founding member of the ANC. In 1909, Mapikela had been part of a multiracial delegation that travelled to London on a failed mission to persuade Parliament not to allow the Afrikaners defeated in the Anglo-Boer war to institutionalise racism. The ANC history recounts that Mapikela was joined in Bloemfontein in 1912 by black African luminaries of the time: Sol Plaatje, a writer and newspaper editor, Alfred Mangena, one of South Africa's first black barristers, and Charlotte Maxeke, an American-educated teacher.

'In their number,' the account of that founding meeting continues, 'there were also royal personages, whose forebears had led the armies that resisted the occupation and seizure of the lands of our continent during the 18th and 19th centuries: Solomon kaDinizulu, Montsioa of the Barolong, Lewanika of the Lozi of Zambia, Letsie II of Lesotho, Labotsibeni from Swaziland, Dalindyebo of the baThembu, Sekhukhuni of the baPedi and Khama from Botswana.'[25]

They had all been summoned by Pixley ka Isaka Seme, a black lawyer who brought a determined intelligence and a love of learning to the struggle against colonialism and apartheid. Seme would lead the ANC in the 1930s. He had left South Africa at the age of 17 to attend Mount Hermon School and Columbia University, New York, and then Oxford.

Seme had spent almost half his life studying abroad when he returned to South Africa in 1911 at the age of 30. When I think of the later university leaders at UFS whose own stories were influenced by journeys abroad, and who would come to see educational travel as a way of preparing students of all races to learn, transform and lead, I consider that Seme's view of the world and his place in it must have been shaped by the opportunity to study outside South Africa. Seme was just the kind of educated black man Afrikaners saw as a threat to their dominance and to the logic of apartheid.

A key element of apartheid was engineering an education system that would ensure there were few black people like Seme. In the 1950s, the government took over and revised the curricula – dumbing them down – of independent, often missionary-run schools that apartheid's planners accused of fanning the ambitions of black South Africans by overeducating them. George Bizos, the liberal, Greek-born lawyer who would later defend Mandela in apartheid courts, saw the tragedy this meant for ordinary South Africans. In *Odyssey to Freedom*, Bizos writes of teachers and parents trying to supplement the inferior education the white government had designed for black children. Their weekend and afternoon classes, called cultural clubs, were declared illegal. Despite lawyers' efforts, the schools were closed down, and their teachers fined or threatened with jail.

In one case, Bizos was dismayed to find that a young man whom the organisers of a cultural club had thought was a student was in fact a spy sent by the police to gather evidence against a teacher. The teacher had asked Bizos: 'Did police have the right to teach a boy to lie about who he was, where he came from and why he attended the club?' Bizos told him that, in apartheid South Africa, there was nothing that said the police didn't have the right.[26]

Over the generations the result, not surprisingly, was a growing contempt among black South Africans for the education they were being offered. When apartheid ended, the majority of South Africa's citizens were left not only impoverished and angry, but without the skills or expertise to meet the challenges of the 21st century. The leaders, black and white, of institutions like UFS are left to cope with that legacy.

In Bloemfontein, university archivists have found minutes of a 1923 governing-council meeting in which the application of an aspiring black student was recorded. The application was denied.[27] Mixed-race and black postgraduate students were first admitted in 1977. The postgraduates were followed by mixed-race undergraduates in 1985 and black undergraduates in 1988. It was not until 1990 that black students were allowed to live on campus.

Black students began to arrive at UFS in large numbers in the 1990s, only after the legal framework of apartheid had been dismantled. Their presence meant language was again an issue.

On a campus that had stubbornly turned its face away while history was being made during the 1980s, the arrival of black students in the 1990s must have felt abrupt and challenging. Change was being ushered in, in the form of fellow South Africans who, it seems, only yesterday could never have aspired to be more than labourers on the white-owned farms.

3. Fragile bridges

Early leaders of the institution that would become UFS include men I think of as language revolutionaries, like D. F. Malherbe, a pioneering novelist in Afrikaans who was also rector of Grey University College at the start of the 20th century. Among leaders moulded at the institution are politicians who championed apartheid, like C. R. Swart, who was both the last Governor General of the Union of South Africa and the first state president of the Republic of South Africa. As minister of justice after the National Party won the elections in 1948, Swart helped draft white rule into law.

As apartheid finally ended in the last decade of the 20th century, some at the university were embracing new ideas about leadership, and selecting leaders who could build bridges from the university's racist policies to a multiracial, democratic future for the institution. In speaking to two of these men who became UFS rectors, I came to understand that the university needed Afrikaner leaders to take those first steps, because the institution needed bridges to connect an isolated Afrikaner community to the broader world.

Apartheid was three years dead when Stef Coetzee, an economist hailing from an old Afrikaner family who had publicly opposed apartheid decades before, took up the challenge of leading the once all-white university. It was during Coetzee's tenure as rector from 1997 to 2002 that the university became the University of the Free State. As Coetzee took over, black students were starting to arrive in large numbers. Administrators like Billyboy Ramahlele and Benito Khotseng remember Coetzee as a man who earnestly and doggedly led some of the first attempts at changing the university.

Coetzee had travelled to Britain in 1980 on leave from his first job in Bloemfontein as a researcher at an institute for social and economic research at the university he would later lead. He had earned his bachelor's and master's degree at Stellenbosch University, and his doctorate at the University of the Orange Free State. As an Afrikaner, he had divorced himself from mainstream Afrikanerdom in the 1980s, adding his voice to those calling for negotiations with the ANC. In the late 1990s, with the ANC in power, the Afrikaner old guard needed leaders like Coetzee, who says he had been inspired as a young scholar to dream of a democratic future for his country after reading a history of the ANC while studying abroad, at the University of Manchester.

'Remember, South Africa was not a democracy then,' Coetzee recalls of the time of his sabbatical in Manchester. 'There's no way of denying it, if you're a scholar of the social sciences. We had a very limited democracy.' For him, just to experience British democracy was revelatory, he says.

Far from the censorship imposed at home by the white minority government, Coetzee found in Manchester University's library a book on the history of the ANC, which was banned in South Africa. It was an organisation he knew little about, one that his government labelled terrorist.

Coetzee had been raised to think of Afrikaners as pioneers, as proud nationalists who had fought for their rights in the face of British colonialism. He recognised a kindred spirit in the stories of the black anti-apartheid activists he found in that library far from home. Afrikaners had bravely fought the British in the Anglo-Boer War, against colonialism, explains Coetzee. 'The British were threatening their language and their citizenship rights. Yet, after that, they made the terrible mistake of doing exactly the same thing to black people that the British had done to the Afrikaner – by not extending democracy to all people in the country,' he says.

That evening, he thought it would be a good idea for his wife, the daughter of a National Party politician, to relax with a glass of wine or two before he told her of his Damascus moment among the books. He wasn't sure whether she would divorce him for it. He told her that the ANC had a remarkable history and that there was a strong resemblance between black African nationalism and Afrikaner nationalism – one fighting British colonialism, the other fighting colonialism and apartheid. 'Unless the two streams of nationalism can find a middle ground and negotiate a settlement, I'm afraid we're going to have a bloodbath here that will simply demolish the country,' he told her.

Coetzee's wife did not divorce him; she stood with him.

Today, Coetzee is sandy-haired and retired, living in an upmarket Cape Town suburb. He occasionally consults on change management for banks and other corporations – a specialism he learnt the hard way.

Before he went to Britain, he tells me, Coetzee described himself as *verlig*, the Afrikaans word for 'enlightened' – he even writes it down in my notebook to underscore its importance. After his time in England, he said, he became a liberal, something more than enlightened, and not a coveted label among Afrikaners. He had committed himself to peace and negotiations, he says.

The Manchester experience changed his whole outlook very suddenly, he says:

> To this day, I hold that moment very dearly – it was when I started to see my country differently. When I read what the ANC were saying and where they were [ideologically speaking], I started to understand their position. And I said, 'My goodness, how is it possible that I haven't seen it before?' It gave me a lot of insight into my own country.

The National Party began talking to Mandela, very much in secret, in the late 1980s, once spiriting him out of prison for a meeting with President P. W. Botha. After Botha resigned in 1989 – months after meeting Mandela – and F. W. de Klerk became the National Party's undisputed leader, momentum for change began to build in earnest. On 2 February 1990, De Klerk opened Parliament with a speech that signalled the beginning of the end of apartheid. Coetzee took his own small steps to encourage debate among Afrikaners about apartheid by forming a discussion group called the Development Society of South Africa when he got back from Manchester. The change was historic and dramatic, says Coetzee:

> How many countries do we know where, first of all, a small group of people gave up power and, secondly, they negotiated the future? The two sides, erstwhile enemies, really negotiated and brokered a Constitution that is still standing today, and which is heralded as one of the best in the world. There's a lot to be proud of. History can be very powerful.

In 1997 his name was among about a dozen or so presented to the committee of professors who would choose the university rector. His liberalism was well known, and must have played a role in his selection. Coetzee says the professors who voted for him told him he had three priorities: 'Transformation, transformation and transformation.'

Coetzee tells me he found that all of the things he had read about at the University of Manchester were, all of a sudden, there. 'I had the opportunity at the university to help establish a democracy,' he says. 'That is how I saw it: we had to establish a democracy on this campus.'

The population of the Free State province was 80 per cent black; the university was less than 40 per cent black when Coetzee took up his post as rector. He envisioned a campus that would one day have many more black students and staff than white. To my mind, the idea that he could even imagine such a possibility, let alone set about realising it, makes him distinct from so many of the university heads who had come before.

'We had to create a new University of the Free State,' he says. 'You had a good, solid university offering good degrees, and with areas of research excellence, and it was far underutilised because it had been for the white minority only. I thought to myself about those potential students who were not getting this education, about what we could do to change their future, and the future of the country.'

Coetzee believes that, from a human development point of view, apartheid had served the country very badly: 'Just think where we could have been if we had started in the 1950s investing in human development like we're doing today, if far more black people had come through the school system and entered universities.'

Years after completing his spell as the university's rector, Coetzee can point to black men and women who were students in his days and who went on to become prominent politicians and high-ranking civil servants in the Free State. Educating black people was the new historic role that the university had to adopt, according to Coetzee.

Coetzee's doctorate thesis was on the development challenges faced by Qwaqwa, which had been starved of resources under apartheid. His research focus and his upbringing among impoverished rural whites in the Northern Cape helped him identify with young black students arriving at the university. He empathised with their understandable sense of alienation; he could see through their eyes how they must have felt about, for example, the campus buildings named after, and statues erected to, Afrikaner heroes. As a young researcher, he had had many opportunities to speak with black people in the townships and the rural areas:

US
South

> I learnt a lot from that experience. As a developmentalist, I understood the country and the nature of the challenges. My generation of developmental economists in this country may have been mostly white, but we knew the development problems inside out – the unemployment, poverty, inequality problems of our country.

As a university leader, he says, you don't have to be a politician, but you need to have political (or sociopolitical) savvy:

> I'm not a politician. But I think I did understand the political context of the country very well. I knew what the challenges were. I understood the particular position of the black students, having come from a very poor background myself. I grew up in the Northern Cape, a poor, white area. So, I knew about poverty from my own childhood. I can never pretend that I could feel it like the black students. But I understood the black students' situation, because I was born at the time when the Afrikaners were still in the poor white era.

Coetzee spoke out for increased government spending on loans and advocated other steps to help impoverished black students reach their higher-education goals. He formed an organisation called the Broad Transformation Forum, which included black and white students and staff, and representatives of groups from on as well as off campus. The forum sat for 18 months, and was charged with drawing up new policies in a range of areas, including how to ensure the campus environment – the buildings and statues – was welcoming to all. Inclusivity was Coetzee's mantra. And that meant drawing in the conservative whites who had once rejected him. He says he was very proud of how the members of the forum could come together in that way and communicate with one another.

Coetzee's main strength as a manager is his ability to galvanise people: 'To mobilise them for a bigger idea. To lead them through a period of paradigm shift. In Afrikaans, we have this expression, "*om 'n kopskuif te maak*", which, translated literally, means "to shift your head".'

To give an example, one evening Coetzee was heading in to an auditorium to address a group of conservative white South Africans who called themselves the Parents' Association. Coetzee chuckles at the name: he believes the association provided little in the way of parental guidance. The head of campus security tried to stop Coetzee from entering, saying he had been tipped off that someone would try to shoot the rector during the meeting. Coetzee went in anyway, along with his whole (integrated) management team. Says Coetzee:

I spoke for 45 minutes, absolutely bluntly, about the new higher-education policy and the demographic facts. And the interesting thing was, they were dead silent. I think many of them heard the full story for the first time that day. And instead of shooting me, they started to ask questions, and more questions. Eventually, I invited them to be part of the Broad Transformation Forum. Within a month, they were in my office, asking how to participate. I got them in. I could have chosen to disregard or ignore them – a bunch of right-wingers that I didn't want to be there. But they were a reality on the campus.

Coetzee also faced opposition from black students and staff. Some were disappointed that a black leader had not been appointed. Others were sceptical about whether Coetzee, despite his reformist credentials, was really committed to change. After all, he was the son of an old Afrikaner family and had come to this university from a high-ranking administrative post at what was then Potchefstroom University for Christian Higher Education, an institution with a reputation for being even more conservative and isolated than the University of the Orange Free State.

Black student protests occasionally flared into violence during Coetzee's time. At one point, he had to call in the police and students were arrested. He had no choice, although it pained him to see students locked up. However, Coetzee's determination to reach out to everyone did not waver. But, he adds, reaching out did not mean compromising his vision: 'I was always clear on where I thought the university was going. Everybody knew that we were serious about transformation.'

He remembers the day, more than a year into his tenure, when a conservative white student leader told him that he and his group wanted to take part in the Broad Transformation Forum. The same day, a radical black student leader also pledged his commitment to the forum. Coetzee says that he celebrated that night.

Another time, during a discussion about the university's core documents that would spell out its culture, Coetzee listened to a black student who was a supporter of the ANC – an organisation reviled by many white South Africans during the apartheid years as a group of godless terrorists. The student asked that the document should include a reference to God. And, ironically, a white student, who happened to be the daughter of a Dutch Reformed Church *dominee*, spoke out for the need for government institutions such as state universities to be secular.

'That was one of the days I would always look back on and say "meaningful things are happening here",' Coetzee says.

He explains that it was a very tense period on campus: 'If we hadn't acted wisely and prudently, it would have gone totally off the rails. Fortunately, due to the sanity that prevailed, it got back on track.'

He credits the Broad Transformation Forum with creating stability on campus, and with that a chance for progress. But Coetzee admits that integrating the residences was a particularly tough challenge. Towards the end of his tenure, he called for at least a third of the places in each residence to be occupied by students of a race other than the majority race in the residence. White students may have read that as a tacit agreement that they could continue to dominate, though Coetzee had actually envisaged it as a first step towards full integration. At any rate, it appears the policy was not closely monitored, and residences ended up segregated again. Students recruited members of their own communities to their residences, effectively taking over housing placement, the job of administrators. Coetzee explains his cautious approach on the residences as one of taking it stepwise so the whole issue didn't explode. 'Looking back,' he says, 'maybe we should have been bolder and just declared that the residences have to be open to all and integrated, and that's it.'

Ramahlele remembers Coetzee's five years as exhilarating, and Coetzee as a leader 'who had a transformative vision for UFS, who really won the support and confidence of black and white students'.

Coetzee appointed Ramahlele director for diversity and equity, a task Ramahlele pursued by working to get people at the university to speak with one another, and to imagine what a truly integrated university might look like.

I ask Ramahlele a difficult question: What went wrong after the campus appeared to have settled into a calm under Coetzee? To buy time, he resorts to a disarming rumble of laughter. Then, he gives his frank appraisal: 'I think there was weak management. Students saw the gap, and students took over.'

When Coetzee stepped down due to ill health in 2002, a new rector was appointed and there was another push to integrate the university. Frederick Fourie was, like Coetzee a well-known Afrikaner liberal. He is also an economist, and, at a time when the university was in financial trouble, that may have been as important in gaining support for his appointment as the expectation that he would, like his predecessor, pursue transformation, transformation and transformation.

Fourie held the post of rector from 2003 to 2008. To discuss those years, Fourie scheduled an appointment with me at Oliewenhuis, an art gallery on a hill once known for its wild olive trees. It is across town from the university, where he is now teaching as a professor.

I find it a vibrantly forward-looking setting for a conversation about the past. The museum has a core of work by contemporary South African artists – black and white – that was returned to South Africa in 2006 from Switzerland, where a collector had taken it. But it is a setting rooted in history.

The Neo-Dutch-style mansion housing the Oliewenhuis Art Museum was built in 1941 as the residence of the Governor General, the chief representative of the Crown when South Africa was still part of the British Empire. King George VI, his wife, and daughters, Elizabeth and Margaret, stayed at Oliewenhuis for three days during a 1947 royal visit to South Africa. When South Africa became an independent republic in 1961, Oliewenhuis hosted its presidents when they visited Bloemfontein. After lobbying by Bloemfontein's art lovers, President P. W.

Botha handed over the grand white building to the National Museum in 1985.

Fourie's own history is rooted in Bloemfontein. He attended Bloemfontein's elite Grey College, an institution that is as much a pillar of the community as the university. Grey College is modelled on the English public school, complete with a coat of arms, a Latin motto and a distinctive handshake by which alumni can recognise one another.

Fourie's father taught at the university, where the young Fourie completed his undergraduate and master's degrees. He was just 29, back from studying for his doctorate in economics at Harvard, when he became a professor at what was then the University of the Orange Free State in 1982.

Fourie was appointed head of the economics department in 1992. In 1997 he followed in his father's footsteps when he became dean of the Faculty of Economic and Management Science, where he established a business school during his tenure. In 1999 he was appointed as vice-rector in charge of academic programmes across the university. He was made rector in 2003.

His career path may seem like the steady rise of an insider. However Fourie remembers it as much more complicated than that. His father was an Afrikaner from the Free State who had sided with Jan Smuts in his support of Britain in World War II. South Africa's involvement in the war sharply divided Afrikaners. Fourie's father fought in the Allied Forces, interrupting his studies in Bloemfontein to do so, and supported Smuts's United Party, a decision that was anathema to Afrikaner nationalists.

Years later, when Fourie was teaching in Bloemfontein, he too was viewed as an outsider. 'I was seen as a rebel, I suppose, at that time,' recalls a trim and greying Fourie, casual yet professorial in cargo pants and blazer. He and a like-minded professor at the time were seen as Marxists – 'lefties and communists. You name it. That was how the times were. I wasn't a political radical. I was just asking questions,' he explains. 'I always asked questions. I didn't like this culture of not asking questions.'

Fourie admits that he doesn't know how he actually became rector: 'I wasn't in the in group of the university community.' He makes a point of telling me he had not been a member of the Broederbond, a powerful secret organisation, which Allister Sparks describes as the 'inner body of Afrikanerdom's ... political intelligentsia where the actual ideological groundwork was laid for apartheid'.[28]

The 'in group' may have thought they were getting a liberal face for the university. What they did get was a leader who applied the same academic rigour that he brought to solving economic problems to the challenge of fundamentally changing the university he, and his father before him, had served, and the university where his children would study.

When he had returned to his alma mater as a professor in 1982, Fourie found that students lived in a 'cocoon' on campus, and this state of affairs wasn't different from other predominantly Afrikaans universities at the time. Urban, English institutions like the University of Cape Town and the University of the Witwatersrand were roiling with political debate. Fourie tells me how leaders of the Bloemfontein branches of the national student organisation would return from national and regional meetings describing 'these wild people from UCT and Wits talking about the Freedom Charter'. Fourie's students did not know what the Freedom Charter was.

In the early 1980s, Fourie and another professor designed a course for economics graduate students that was attended by many younger student leaders. The two professors wanted to help their charges understand the ideas they'd heard discussed by their counterparts elsewhere in the country. Says Fourie:

> We were trying to expose those students, the leadership at least, to a broader world of ideas and people than they would have encountered locally. We had them read the Freedom Charter; we had them read different historical perspectives on South African history: Afrikaner, English liberal, Marxist, ANC and labour-union perspectives. We let them read different ideological perspectives on the political economy: rightist and leftist, everything. We were trying to unfreeze their minds.

While a small number of academics were trying to prepare their students for the inevitable, others were lending their scholarship to the state. George Bizos describes in his memoirs how he confronted expert witnesses from the University of the Orange Free State during trials intended to weaken the anti-apartheid United Democratic Front by sending its leaders to Robben Island. The university was 'conferring doctorates on the theory of "revolutionary warfare"', Bizos writes. 'These studies sought to explain why legitimate political activity elsewhere in the world was treated as treason or terrorism in South Africa.'[29]

He describes an expert from the university, André Pruis, being called by prosecutors in one of the most closely watched, and longest, trials of the 1980s – the Delmas Treason Trial. Twenty-two men, among them top United Democratic Front leaders, were accused of working with alleged co-conspirators, including then Bishop Desmond Tutu, to foment violence in the Vaal Triangle and other parts of South Africa. They were charged with treason, terrorism and working for the then banned ANC. In court, Bizos recalls, Pruis 'spoke of how organisations professing to be nonviolent brought about a revolutionary climate by criticising the government, its policies and structures and by discrediting as collaborators those who served the government'.[30]

Bizos writes of forcing Pruis, who went on to become a Deputy National Police Commissioner in post-apartheid South Africa, to admit ignorance of historical figures and of the theories of the foreign revolutionaries he claimed to have studied.[31]

The Pruis described by Bizos embodies the danger of scholarship in isolation and underlines the importance of what men like Coetzee and Fourie would try to do – not just help their university break free from the constraints of racism, but to adopt a stance of leadership in a fast-changing world.

Fourie also brought ideas for renewal at a time of economic crisis for his institution. His campaign included small, personal steps. Fourie, who has an unconscious habit of touching a conversation partner lightly on the shoulder when something is said that reveals a connection has been made, says he tried to break his own social patterns. He would just 'go and chat with black colleagues during tea breaks, not white colleagues; talk about everyday stuff; get to know each other; sit in the sun and talk nonsense. It's natural for people to group, to coalesce amongst their own.'

Some unexpected and revealing encounters served as reminders that apartheid's divisions were over more than just racial lines. While chatting on a road trip, Fourie remembers, it emerged that a certain white staff member had been an anti-apartheid activist in exile. He had sneaked back across the Botswana–South Africa border at a time when a white colleague was a border guard for the apartheid government. At that moment they could have shot at each other. And now they were fellow academics.

'I'll never forget that moment,' Fourie says. 'The realisation amongst all of us of where we were and where we are.'

Fourie set about bringing students, teachers and staff into a campus-wide conversation, in small groups, about where the institution was headed: what values it should espouse, what principles it should adopt and what kind of institution it should be once transformation was complete. He and a colleague from the law faculty drew up a draft institutional charter that Fourie describes as almost like a Constitution and Bill of Rights for the university. For him, the key element was to create the foundations for the growth of a culture in which no group would dominate.

He was inspired, he says, by the spirit of a speech Nelson Mandela had made in 1964 to the court that would sentence him to imprisonment on Robben Island:

> I have fought against white domination, and I have fought against black domination. I have cherished the ideal of a democratic and free society in which all persons live together in harmony and with equal opportunities. It is an ideal for which I hope to live for and to achieve. But if needs be, it is an ideal for which I am prepared to die.[32]

Fourie, whose inauguration as rector was attended by Mandela, said he wanted to create a university at which no one would feel he or she was an outsider. 'Nobody must dominate. There shouldn't be a dominant group or culture or style,' Fourie says. 'These things are easy terms. But it's quite difficult for people to work through them, both black and white.'

The charter was adopted by the University Senate and the University Council in July 2007, part of a larger package aimed at transforming the heart and mind of the institution.

'We spent a couple of years really thinking about transformation,' he says. 'An intellectual and analytical exercise. Asking really hard questions: What is transformation? What is good transformation? What is bad transformation?'

A task team devised a 34-page transformation plan that set goals and deadlines, and assigned managers to projects ranging, for example, from ensuring all students were made welcome in university choirs to changing the languages in which classes were taught, the way meetings were held, the criteria by which curricula were designed.

'We had a comprehensive plan affecting every bit of the university,' he says. 'Well considered, well thought out. You'd think that, at a university, a good analytical argument would carry the day, but when it comes to emotional or race politics, it very often does not.'

They may be brick-and-mortar structures, but the halls of residence at UFS have always held great symbolic weight. In retrospect, Fourie's plans to integrate the residences read like a footnote. The plan envisaged residence integration as among several strategies for using 'diversity as a source of enrichment of students' educational and personal development'.[33] The policy was to be phased in. For example, a hostel where most residents were white would have to have at least 30 per cent non-white residents by 2008, while one that was predominantly black would have to have at least 30 per cent white residents by 2008. The goal was for each residence to be 50 per cent white and 50 per cent black by 2010.

Fourie wanted residences to become places where students from segregated communities, schools and churches would be re-socialised in a diverse environment, in preparation for living, working and taking leadership roles in a multiracial society. It was a major challenge, as Fourie explains:

We couldn't send them out there to the workplace without exposing them to diversity. Otherwise, we'd be doing them a disservice. But these conservative white people never even heard us. The new residence policy was in the interest of their kids' future. But they didn't see it that way. They just labelled the whole initiative 'integration' – a dreaded word in the Afrikaner community – and started a war against it.

Fourie himself had lived as a student in one of the university's most prestigious residences, Abraham Fischer House. He says, without apparent irony, that the initiation rites at Vishuis, as the residence is affectionately known, didn't make much of an impression on him because the two years' compulsory army service he had just completed had toughened him up.

Both his parents had died by the time Fourie reached university, so Vishuis was very much his home. But he does not look back on his years in residence with the warm nostalgia of a true insider. Instead, he remembers being uncomfortable with what he calls the rugby-mad culture of the residence in his day. At Vishuis, he wasn't part of the in group either – he wasn't one of 'the boys' who set the tone in the residence. That was when Fourie started asking questions.

His nonconformist past had not prepared him for the fierce resistance he would encounter when he attempted to integrate the residences more than 30 years later. He says he saw resistance mounting, so he met with conservative political groups on and off campus whom he saw as leading the opposition to his policy to increase diversity in the residences. At the time, Fourie says, people at the university liked to talk about transformation – but only as long as nothing changed. He believes that when he proposed the policy that residences would be integrated, the white, mostly Afrikaner, community – including some members of the University Council – suddenly realised that he meant to do more than write plans.

'The residence policy signalled that we really intended to change the dominant institutional culture of the campus, and of residences in particular,' he says. 'For most white Afrikaner parents and alumni, the residence was an important symbol, a last line of resistance.'

The infamous Reitz video brought the fierceness of this resistance into the open. Fourie says the video was produced a couple of months after the new policy was approved by the university administration, at a time when the Freedom Front Plus, a conservative Afrikaner political party with a student branch at the university, was launching a court challenge to the policy. Fourie says the party 'created a certain legitimacy for open resistance, helped create an atmosphere, especially in the male residences, that serious resistance to the university authorities is okay. The Reitz video was produced in this atmosphere.'

The video was purportedly made for a hostel event, a 'cultural evening', according to newspaper reports at the time. Ramahlele, who, when the video was made, had risen from being head of a residence to the position of a senior university manager charged with transformation, believes it was more than that. He claims white students from Reitz had organised a competition to see who could best illustrate their opposition to living alongside black students. Ramahlele tells me it is likely that there were a number of multimedia entrants, but only one surfaced. It was posted on YouTube and was viewed around the world, setting off a scandal in early 2008.

The video starts innocuously enough, with scenes of the exterior of the Reitz building. Cleaners at the residence then appear in the ubiquitous blue overalls of black workers across South Africa. White students wearing jeans and golf shirts put the cleaners through a parody of a residence initiation ceremony. There are drinking games and dancing. Women cleaners, ungainly but game, are filmed passing a rugby ball and struggle down an athletics track. There may be scenes of laughter, but any South African will see in the video the traditional pattern of power and subservience – the black workers at the mercy of the younger white men.

Then comes the scene that has shocked the world. The camera closes in on a bowl of stew, then pulls back to show a white student taking it into a bathroom, placing it on a toilet seat and, with his back to the camera, apparently urinating in the food. In the next scene, the workers crouch on the ground and are served the stew. More laughter.

The video ends with the black cleaners being invited to move into the residence, and a strapline in Afrikaans reads: 'This is what we really think of racial integration.'

The video may be tame compared with the violence the university experienced in the 1990s. Nonetheless, the stew imagery recalls the sandwiches spiked with laxatives that sparked a near riot on the campus in 1997. When food is placed before us, we interpret it as an offer of nourishment and an acknowledgement of shared humanity. That makes the betrayal all the deeper when the food is poisoned, either literally or psychologically.

Perhaps the most troubling aspect of the video in the minds of the university administrators, however, including Ramahlele and Khotseng, who had experienced the worst periods of racial tension at the university, was the hard-to-escape conclusion that attitudes had not changed despite all their efforts.

The laxatives had sent a few students to the hospital. The video, in which relatively little is said, has a language of imagery that is much more powerful than words. And its message was sent around the world.

As a journalist, I have pored over survey results about racial attitudes among South Africans. I have interviewed white South Africans who did not realise they were revealing racist thinking when they told me, a black American, that 'our blacks' are different from 'you Americans'. They thought that was a compliment. In the time-honoured tradition of gathering the opinions of 'ordinary people' for articles, I have greeted strangers on the streets of South Africa to request impromptu interviews. Some white strangers would walk stiffly past, staring coldly somewhere over my head. But until I watched the Reitz video, I had never had the opportunity to see the world unfiltered through the eyes of a racist.

It's not just that the black residence cleaning staff are depicted in stereotypical ways. The white students themselves are stereotypes – all that are missing are the knee socks and sjamboks. It is as if they lack the courage to depict themselves more imaginatively, to consider that the traditions they have been given are malleable.

Is it fear that led these young men to flee into self-caricature? What would it take to ease them out of the prison they had built for themselves, into a wider world? Those universal questions, and the sense of glimpsing a dark human secret, are what made the video newsworthy across South Africa and around the world. When I arrived for my assignment in South Africa, too late to report on much more than the aftermath of the video, I was intrigued by these questions.

Former rector Stef Coetzee tells me that learning of the Reitz video hit him harder than anything he had experienced during his own tenure. This from a man who had to call in the police to control rioting students, a man who served just one five-year term, stepping down in 2002 because leading the university had taken such a toll on his health.

In part, the force of his reaction to the video was seeing that the past still lived on, that that sort of old-style humour was still prevalent among students, he says. The shock of the Reitz video lay in realising that all the bridges between cultures that he and others had worked to erect were so fragile. And Coetzee knows that, had his luck been different, such an incident could well have exploded during his tenure.

'Transformation never stops,' Coetzee concludes. 'It goes on and on and on.'

After the Reitz video scandal, Fourie resigned. His health, like Coetzee's before him, had also suffered. Looking back, Fourie says that lack of support in the university community, personal attacks in the local press and even threats to his life had drained him:

> I had no emotional or intellectual energy left. I suddenly knew I couldn't take it further. I had done what I could. I had succeeded in getting the university across the bridge. You felt like a Churchill after the war. I thought, in terms of leadership, the university needed a new face, new energy, new ideas. We had crossed the bridge. But we needed a new voice to take the process into the next phase of transformation and to implement the policies, including residence-integration policies.

Amid an international uproar, the four student videographers were expelled and their university launched a court case against them. When I speak to Afrikaners about the video, I sense they feel shame. The Reitz students eventually apologised to the black cleaners as part of a reconciliation effort spearheaded by the university authorities and others. Perhaps they also owe an apology to fellow Afrikaners, who felt, by association, humiliated by the stereotypes perpetuated on tape.

4. A knowledge of apartheid

Magon Mouton took on a challenge when she decided to become a Kovsie. She would face rejection at UFS because of her dark skin. But, at the same time, she would be embraced because of who she is – an actress, a musician, an enthusiastic sampler of cultures and ideas, a sympathetic listener and an insightful observer.

Mouton, a drama and psychology student from the Northern Cape, had just arrived at UFS when its new top executive, rector Jonathan Jansen, took the bold step of forgiving the white students who had humiliated the black cleaning staff with the Reitz video, announcing the move in his inaugural address, delivered in October 2009. Jansen was sharply criticised by some for this, but Mouton saw Jansen's gesture as akin to a father taking responsibility for a child's mistake. She believes that the videographers were first and foremost young boys, students, and that it was the university's responsibility to try to help them see that what they had done was wrong, and at the same time to show that we can all learn from our mistakes.

Mouton believes that Jansen leads an administration that has taken on the unenviable task of teaching students their responsibilities in a recently democratic, multiracial South Africa. By establishing a special programme known as F1 (for first year),

Jansen has made students – including Mouton – part of that project. F1 is an overseas-study programme for first-year students, also known as Leadership for Change. Its goal is to broaden students' knowledge, to influence them for good.

And the challenge is not unique to UFS: Mouton refers to friends she has at the University of Stellenbosch, the premier Afrikaans university where her mother and other relatives studied, and at the North-West University (formerly the Potchefstroom University for Christian Higher Education, another prominent institution with Afrikaans roots). She says that neither Stellenbosch nor North-West University is free from racial flare-ups, citing stories she has heard from friends:

> There have been some incidents at those universities that are mind-blowing, but, for some reason, they just never seem to capture the media's attention. Because this is the Free State, and because it's Afrikaans, people assume that Kovsies have a lot of ground to make up. But it's actually a lot worse at other universities. And you don't see people there trying to change it, trying to start something new: they just sit back and let it happen. When we Kovsies see a problem, we try to fix it.

Mouton was born the year before South Africa's first all-race elections. She is vivacious and optimistic – but that optimism has been tested. Under the former racial definitions of apartheid, she is coloured; her high-school boyfriend (he was head boy and she was head girl) was a white Afrikaner. What seemed to them like a straightforward relationship became far from simple when they both enrolled at UFS.

Mouton explains how her boyfriend ended up in a traditional res that still remains a hotbed of resistance to integration, despite all the changes UFS has undergone. His older housemates were on his case a lot. 'They're like, "You're a white boy. You're an Afrikaans boy. Why are you dating this mixed-race girl?"' she says.

They would meet at the Bridge, the university social centre where students can grab a beer or recharge their cellphones. But they would arrive separately to avoid attracting attention. In that situation, she felt rejected:

> We weren't really accepted. People like to say that you shouldn't be defined by what people say or think about you. But when you're a first year, you kind of have to follow the seniors. You have to observe the traditions of your residence. I wasn't mature enough at that stage to handle all the gossiping and staring.

The couple broke up early in their second year, not long after Mouton returned from the F1 trip abroad, the objective of which is to help UFS students navigate a new world at home, where the rules about how races relate to one another are changing so fast that many cannot cope with the transformation.

Looking back, Mouton says she and her boyfriend might have drifted apart anyway – after all, high-school romances don't usually last. She says that her attitude to the pressure they were under as an interracial couple has matured, even if the attitude of others has not:

> I'm more comfortable in my own skin. I know what I believe. Because of my experiences on this campus over the past year, and because F1 broadened my horizons and taught me to accept people for who they are and accept who I am, I feel that I'm more mature now, more able to withstand people's gossiping and staring and laughing.

It seems to me that Mouton has come to a point where she can forgive herself for not holding on to her relationship in the face of racist opposition. And forgiving ourselves takes particular courage.

Jansen, the 13th rector of UFS, who was appointed after Fourie had resigned, is the first black person to have held that position in the university's century-plus history. A round-faced man in round glasses, Jansen has a rhetorical style that combines academic prose with well-timed outbursts of humour and plain speaking. He's like a favourite uncle with a very big brain.

In his 2009 inaugural address at the university, Jansen looked back more than a century to a meeting held in Bloemfontein to try to avert the Anglo-Boer War. The talks failed, and, as he said in his speech, 'the failure to reconcile at such a crucial time as that left scars on the South African political psyche to this day. And I have no doubt that the single most important reason for the breakdown in the Bloemfontein Conference was, profoundly, a failure of leadership.'[34]

As the new head of the university, Jansen believes he had no choice but to take responsibility for what the four white Reitz students had done, and he asked for people's forgiveness.

'I apologise to every black person on this campus and in this province for our long history of exclusion and marginalisation of black people within this institution. I apologise to every decent white citizen of our university that you were shamed by the Reitz incident,' he said in his inaugural address.

In the same address, however, Jansen announced that he was offering the students who had been expelled for making the Reitz video a chance to study again at UFS, and he dropped the university's own court case against them. In a separate criminal case, which ended in 2010, the four former UFS students pleaded guilty to charges of *crimen injuria* and were fined R20 000 each. In 2011 another case, brought by the Human Rights Commission, ended with a meeting between the members of the cleaning staff who had been humiliated and the former students. During the meeting, the black elders told the young white men: 'We have forgiven you. Now you must forgive yourselves.'

The Human Rights Commission also announced at the time that it had helped broker a settlement agreement the provisions of which included the establishment of a think tank on human rights and reconciliation at UFS.[35]

Jansen believes there is no better place for such an institution than in South Africa, with its history of embarking on a national truth and reconciliation effort. South Africa, he tells me, represents 'an example of how to be counter-intuitive in your politics. That is a lesson that, with all our difficulties, we can offer the world'.

White UFS students and professors continued to argue over whether too much attention had been paid to the video, which in a way started the university on its own counter-intuitive path. They debated whether the video deserved all the media coverage and even whether urine had in reality been splashed over the stew.

Black South Africans, for their part, were outraged by Jansen's gesture of reconciliation, saying he was appeasing racists and failed to recognise the damage they had done. But Jansen was not playing down the video. And his stance earned him praise from well-known black South Africans, among them Archbishop Emeritus Desmond Tutu, who is sometimes called the conscience of South Africa. Tutu issued an open letter offering Jansen support in which he wrote that 'revenge and retribution are easy. Forgiveness is not for sissies'.[36]

Mothusi Lepheane, a lawyer from Johannesburg, was working in Bloemfontein at the time as head of the local branch of the national Human Rights Commission. He had been advising the black cleaners caught up in the Reitz incident. He tells me how shocked and dismayed they were by Jansen's gesture, and that he wishes he had had some warning that it was coming. But, in time, he came to embrace Jansen's move. He points out that there is nowhere for the four white Reitz students to go: 'We don't have a camp or university for racists. Bring them back; let them learn how to live with' other people.

The video, Jansen tells me, which is available on YouTube to be watched over and over again, hit a number of cultural belief systems in the stomach. 'First of all, there's the obvious black-white thing. Then there's the young-old thing. And then there's the gender aspect. It hits the senses in a way nothing else can,' he says.

But he blames a whole system, and the men and women who had created and fostered it for generations before the young men were born, for the conditions that made the video possible. In that light, the video itself was not the crime, so it makes sense that Jansen felt the four young men had been made scapegoats. Jansen sought a teaching moment.

During a campus ceremony in 2011, the Reitz students gave a public apology, which was accepted by the black cleaners. Jansen inaugurated the International Institute for Studies in Race, Reconciliation and Social Justice at UFS. The institute is charged with doing research and starting a dialogue aimed at providing an understanding of what led to the Reitz incident, and to help provide tools for managing diversity.

Jansen was not all about forgiveness, however. He pressed ahead rapidly to racially integrate the campus residences. He described the phased plan that had been in place when he arrived as 'fake' (namely, to go from a ratio of white students to those of other races of 70:30 and then to 50:50). He insisted on at least 50:50 racial integration immediately for incoming students. 'I stood up and said, "This is what's going to happen."' Students who objected were told simply: 'If you want to study here, then you're going to have to learn to live together,' Jansen tells me.

Jansen also joined a long line of rectors who have tried to end the worst excesses of the UFS reses. In his inaugural address, he declared illegal the *ontgroening* (initiation ceremonies) practised in some halls of residence. 'Any senior student who lays his hand on a first-year student will not only be brought before a disciplinary committee of the university, but will face criminal prosecution in the courts,' he said. 'The mindless rituals that treat first-year students as children and seniors as parents will be replaced by gradually building a new institutional and residential culture.'[37]

I first met Jansen not long after that speech, which I found extraordinary enough to make me think he would be a good subject for an Associated Press profile. I had 'stalked' him before travelling to Bloemfontein to meet him: I read his books and newspaper columns, and attended readings and speeches he gave in Johannesburg.

For the profile interview, which turned out to be the first of many talks we were to have over the years, we sat down in his high-ceilinged office. Then we walked across the university campus and I marvelled at how often he would stop to chat with students and staff. No one seemed intimidated by him. (His staff complain about how difficult it is to start meetings on time with him when he chooses to walk around the campus.)

Jansen and I have talked about the hard line he has taken towards racial integration at UFS, and whether his predecessors could have been firmer. Jansen believes he was able to take steps that the Afrikaner rectors could not, because he was not risking censure from his own community.

To illustrate this, his inaugural address was dedicated to Bram Fischer, a graduate of the university and son of a respected Afrikaner family. A campus residence is named after Fischer's father, who was once chief jurist in the Orange Free State. Fischer's grandfather was prime minister in the Orange River Colony, as the once independent Boer republic was known after the Anglo-Boer War.

Bram Fischer broke his Afrikaner ranks to become a communist. He befriended Nelson Mandela, defended him in court and fought for the rights of black South Africans. Mandela writes of Bram Fischer in his autobiography, *Long Walk to Freedom*: 'As an Afrikaner whose conscience forced him to reject his own heritage and be ostracised by his own people, he showed a level of courage and sacrifice that was in a class by itself. I fought only against injustice, not my own people.'[38]

Fischer was sentenced in 1965 to life in prison for conspiracy to commit sabotage. He was released early on humanitarian grounds, and died of cancer a few months later, in 1975.

Jansen explains to me that one has to understand the history of the concept of betrayal within Afrikaner society: 'People were executed for this. You still get executed – metaphorically speaking.'

But, for him, that was not a risk.

He tells me of a certain Afrikaner who had held the top university post long before his arrival. He visited Jansen shortly after his appointment to ask him to hold off on racial integration. 'I listened respectfully, and saw him out of my office,' Jansen says.

I believe Jansen also has the advantage of history, of a foundation built by UFS heads like Fourie, Khotseng, Coetzee and Ramahlele. Time has seen the fading away of conservative whites who led the charge against residence integration. And even if their parents might find the idea strange, at least some of the young white students at UFS today are looking for tools to help them navigate a multicultural future.

According to Fourie, Jansen's era is the 'maturation phase' in the university's development. After 12 years of earnest and serious efforts to transform it by instituting rather radical policy changes, Jansen faced the difficult reality of making those – perhaps idealistic – policies actually work in the context of a diverse student population.

Jansen, Fourie says, 'could not have tackled the projects that he did without the foregoing hard transformative work done by his predecessors. And the jury on the Jansen era is still out, of course. Indications are that integration in residences is still an incomplete journey, notably in some historically black residences.'

Fourie is an admirer of Jansen, but he betrays some exasperation when he observes how Afrikaners have accepted Jansen's insistence on integration. 'I was never really accepted by the mainstream Afrikaner community,' Fourie says. 'As a vice chancellor, you can't do things alone. You have to take all the different stakeholders with you. But it was not possible to take the majority of the Afrikaner community in the Free State with me. They saw me as a traitor. When I said it, I was torn apart. When Jansen says it, they accept it.' Strange as it may be, Fourie believes that is how change works, how history works: every leader has his or her particular role.

Coetzee expresses a similar sentiment, noting that when he was appointed as rector, many black students were disappointed that a black candidate had not been selected. He says that he envies Jansen sometimes because he could get things done quickly 'because he's got legitimacy. He came through the struggle era.'

Jansen, who has faced plenty of resistance from black and white South Africans alike, might well raise an eyebrow at such depictions.

When Fourie finished his doctorate at Harvard, the former rector says, he could have taught anywhere in the world, but he chose to come back to Bloemfontein. As we speak in a museum café, Fourie points out the green leg of the table where we are seated. In Europe or the US, he says, cultural and political arguments would revolve around what shade of green the table should be painted. 'Here, we're still constructing the table. To me, constructing the society is more interesting than fine-tuning.' It's hard work, he says, building a society. 'But at least you're doing something.'

Fourie was an Afrikaner outsider among Afrikaners. Jansen is even further from the norm in Bloemfontein, but he is not entirely a stranger – there are some parallels with his own background. Jansen grew up in an evangelical Christian family in Cape Town, and came to Bloemfontein knowing the power of starting a staff meeting with a prayer in this conservative and religious part of central South Africa. And he speaks Afrikaans, often a first or second language for South Africans raised in mixed-race communities.

Although he was born in a coloured community, Jansen identifies himself as black. He was born in 1956, a busy year for apartheid's architects. Laws stripping coloured South Africans of the right to vote went into effect that year. Also enacted then were laws making it easier to reserve certain jobs for whites, ensuring they wouldn't have to compete with black workers and that they would earn higher wages. Under another law passed that year, blacks could be banished from their homes to isolated rural areas.

The year 1956 also saw a march on Pretoria that united thousands of women of all races against the extension to women of the pass laws, which restricted the movement of black South Africans. Women marched under the slogan 'you strike a woman, you strike a rock'.

A year earlier, South Africans of all races had gathered in a muddy field in Kliptown, Soweto, to adopt the Freedom Charter, which proclaimed the then radical idea that 'South Africa belongs to all who live in it, black and white'.

Jansen and his family experienced the brutality and injustice of apartheid. 'I think my grandfather went blind because they took his land away to give it to white people,' he tells me. According to family lore, the man simply refused to see his house being handed over.

As a teenager, Jansen would visit his grandparents in Montagu. On one occasion, as he walked to the shop to buy a loaf of bread, he was hit on the heel by a brick a white boy had thrown at him. A big city boy lacking the submissiveness usually displayed by the rural black community, Jansen rushed at the stone-thrower. The white boy's father, an off-duty police officer, happened to be at home. Jansen remembers being forced into a car and beaten on the way to the police station. Only when an aunt came to plead for his release was he freed.

Jansen studied at the University of the Western Cape, which had been created in 1959 as a separate institution for coloured people. By the 1970s, it was known as a bastion of anti-apartheid activism. Jansen was the first person in his family to acquire a university degree. He became a high-school teacher and taught biology in the Cape Flats, home to families forcibly removed from Cape Town to make way for whites and an area notorious for its gang violence.

Jansen has written about how his own activism developed when he travelled to the US to pursue his postgraduate studies in the 1980s. There he met fellow South Africans who were leaders of student groups allied with the then banned ANC, as well as American students who were pressing their universities to disinvest from companies doing business in apartheid South Africa.

As a young man, Jansen says, he was angered to hear Mandela talk of reconciliation between blacks and whites. The man who would later extend his own reconciliation and forgiveness to the young white men who had made the racist video once told friends that he would never teach at a white institution.

Jansen did his master's at Cornell University and his doctorate at Stanford before returning in the early 1990s to a South Africa that was changing fast. He took up a post at the University of Durban-Westville, which had been founded for South Africans of Indian descent, but was open to black people as well when Jansen arrived. The once angry young man was now a scholar specialising in education. Jansen had begun to worry that the black majority, who had been denied so much under apartheid, would grow impatient with democracy if it did not deliver economic opportunity. He saw education as key, but at Durban-Westville and other institutions, Jansen saw racial resentment derailing attempts to give an impoverished majority the tools it needed to succeed. For Jansen, the Mandela-style reconciliation which he had once scoffed began to look like part of the solution.

In 2000 he found himself working at one of those white institutions he had once held in contempt. He became the first black educator at the University of Pretoria, another historically Afrikaans institution, as dean of students. At Pretoria, he began to develop some of the theories he would later test at UFS.

Today, UFS is led by a man whose exalted title may be rector, but who sees himself as not far removed from the high-school biology classroom where he started his career. 'I've always enjoyed the fact that in this vocation you can make a huge difference simply by influencing students for good,' Jansen says. 'If we succeed, the country succeeds.'

In his inaugural address, he announced he would be establishing the F1 programme, with the goal of broadening students' horizons and thinking about what their society might be:

> The most important challenge is the problem of knowledge. The often troubled knowledge the student comes to the university with – the knowledge of the past, the knowledge of black and white, and, especially, the knowledge of the future. The university curriculum, here and elsewhere, has not yet confronted the crucial question of what a student needs to know in a dangerous and divided world.[39]

When he came to UFS, Jansen knew that change was about more than enforcing new rules and holding public ceremonies. Campaigns for change had previously been led from the top down, with committees, timelines and ambitious plans on paper. Students had not been ignored by earlier leaders at the university, but Jansen brought them closer to the centre of the exercise. He wanted to implement change from the youngest, the newest, upwards.

Jansen also had to tackle the quandary of why young South Africans who had no real memory of apartheid were replicating their parents' approach to race relations. Many young Afrikaners, Jansen knew from his years on the staff at the University of

Pretoria, come from isolated farming communities and small towns. And with the end of apartheid, many had absorbed their parents' uncertainty about their place in a new South Africa, and taken on their sense of fear and loss. They arrived at a university where tradition and conformity were valued, and enforced in the res culture. They were not used to questioning their own choices.

'They come from closed circuits of influence,' Jansen tells me. 'They're used to barking orders at black people. And, suddenly, they're in the same classroom, the same res, with black kids.'

Many of the black students also came from rural areas. Even those who were politicised did not have much experience living and working with white South Africans. Apartheid had seen to that. To counter this, Jansen devised a plan aimed at 'complicating their cultural and linguistic and political lives'. His F1 programme was part of an attempt to get young South Africans to question their own knowledge of themselves and their place in their country, and of their country and its place in the world. He focused on first-year students, fresh from their farms and small towns, as well as from the cities, because they had not yet been moulded by university tradition.

After a rigorous application process, which included essays and interviews, in 2010 he sent 75 first-year students to the US. A group has gone abroad every year since, and by 2013 the F1 participants had grown to 150 students, who were sent to some of the finest universities in Asia, West Africa, Europe and the US.

Jansen wants them to get a first-hand look at how other countries approached the challenge of building multicultural societies. No country has all the answers, but Jansen wants his students to have a taste of possibility. 'You couldn't go to a more optimistic country than the United States,' Jansen says of the country that hosted all his students in 2010 and continues to be a major part of the F1 story. 'My memory of it, as a student and a regular visitor, is that even in the midst of a recession, people talk well of being an American, of the future, and of themselves.'

The students spend just two weeks abroad, but their shaping is far from over when the visit ends. Back in South Africa, they are plunged into a series of discussions and exercises designed to prepare them to share the new ideas and perspectives they have absorbed at their overseas campuses. Attendance at monthly leadership forums is required, as is mentoring first-year students once the F1 students reach their second year. They are asked to work in groups established according to the foreign universities they have visited, each group being required to come up with at least two campus-wide projects designed to pass on what they have learnt.

The F1 programme is at the heart of Jansen's efforts to transform his university. The students are invited – indeed, enjoined – to be part of something bigger than themselves. Jansen tells me: 'Our entire strategy is premised on the fact that the young are more courageous and ambitious and idealistic and hopeful. And with the combination of love and direction, they will get it right.'

In pursuit of his goals, Jansen is doing more than sending students abroad. He has, for example, also tried to encourage independent thinking in the tradition-bound residences, as well as in classrooms, where authoritarianism has long stifled the kind of debate that swept across Western universities decades ago. Jansen's belief is that if students born after apartheid's end can at last start questioning their elders' assumptions, more than just his university will change in the process.

One strategy is to move professors into the reses, where they act as advisers, a role not traditionally played by professors. Another is to poach top professors from more liberal institutions across South Africa. Although UFS is proud of its achievements in several academic fields, among them medicine, law and drama, it's still seen as provincial and isolated in the country's heartland. It lacks the allure of other educational institutions in South Africa, like the English universities UCT and Witwatersrand, and the Afrikaans Stellenbosch. And it has a very low international profile.

If a black man can give them academic prestige, Afrikaners might be willing to concede to his racial-integration campaign. Not that Jonathan Jansen, a careful man for all his blunt language, would put the argument quite in those terms, but he has noted the positive reaction when he has brought world-famous black researchers to teach at the university. 'You will not believe how [academic excellence] undermines racism and racial thinking,' says Jansen. 'I find that to be more effective in dealing with racism than preaching and accusing.'

In his inaugural address, he promised to lead the university very quickly 'to become a national and indeed international centre for academic excellence. Let me be clear that the UFS will be unashamedly elitist in its drive to become an African university instantly recognised for excellence in research, teaching and what my predecessor so beautifully called "engaged scholarship" in relation to the communities around us.'[40]

Certainly, those who founded and nurtured the university believed in the transformative power of education, and had no plans to build a second-rate institution. But a narrow, sometimes defensive, nationalism is also part of the university's history. And, it turns out, isolation does not foster excellence. An institution can have ideology or ideas, and Jansen is pushing for ideas. He has therefore pledged to make the university more rigorous academically and has reached out to poor high schools, those serving black as well as white students, to help them ensure their schoolchildren are ready for the challenge of university.

In 2012, he brought together to UFS students, professors and administrators from several universities around the world, from the US to Japan, to brainstorm with South Africans about how to build a better university. I joined the group, since it offered another chance for me to better understand the university and its goals. Jansen was frank, telling us one evening: 'South Africa and this university are still a work in progress.'

He told the group two stories – one of his own transformation, and another of his audacious optimism. 'I hated white people for a huge part of my life for what they did to my family, and to my grandfather, in particular,' Jansen begins the first story. It is a story that he has told often and it features in his memoir, *Knowledge in the Blood: Confronting Race and the Apartheid Past*. The story takes place at a retreat for teenage girls from a historically Afrikaans high school. Jansen had been invited to give a lecture to the schoolgirls, and describes how the students initially failed to realise that the unknown black visitor was a guest. One girl ordered him to bring her tea, assuming that any black man must be a servant.

Jansen had chosen a biblical theme for his lecture, a way to connect with churchgoing girls from a conservative community. He presented the Parable of the Good Samaritan as a multicultural tale, in which a Samaritan reaches across cultural borders to help a Jew. It is a story, he says, about relating to 'those whom you think are different from you'.

'The hand of a grade 10 girl shoots up for attention,' Jansen relates in his memoir. 'This kind of interruption of an adult is unusual in an Afrikaans school, but I am happy to find response. "Well, professor," she starts. "I agree with what you say about crossing bridges and stuff. But tell me this, how do I cross bridges toward someone who looks like the people who almost killed my sister and me a few weeks ago in a violent car hijacking?"'[41]

Years later, relating this story to the group of foreign visitors I had joined at UFS, Jansen explains how the girl's question had changed him: 'I could no longer see myself as better. I could no longer see myself as the only one hurt. You cannot presume to change others until you change yourself.'

His second story was also about violence and reconciliation, but, this time, the setting was far from home. Jansen asked us to consider Izzeldin Abuelaish, a Palestinian doctor who, the year before, had come to attend the university's think tank on race, reconciliation and social justice. While in Bloemfontein, Abuelaish – whom I had met on an earlier visit to the university – had spoken to students and staff about the day that three of his daughters and a niece were killed by Israelis during their 2009 assault on Gaza in response to Hamas rocket fire.

Abuelaish used to cross the border to Israel and was well known for his work at an Israeli hospital. He partnered with Israeli doctors on research projects, and brought Gazan patients to sophisticated Israeli hospitals for care that they could not get at home.

During the 2009 violence, Abuelaish was also known for speaking to journalists about the impact on innocent Palestinians of the Israeli onslaught meant to root out extremists. The doctor called an Israeli anchor at a Tel Aviv news station after his home had been hit, and his anguished account of the death of his daughters and niece was broadcast live.

Abuelaish went on to write *I Shall Not Hate: A Gaza Doctor's Journey*, in which he says the deaths of his daughters and niece did not shake his belief in the need for love over hate, forgiveness over revenge.

In summing up the story about Abuelaish, Jansen says: 'That is uncommon grace. That is the kind of leadership that I know resides in all of us.'

5. Views from abroad

As the plane took off from Johannesburg for Dubai in September 2011, the dozens of young UFS students aboard raised their arms and cheered. The students cheered again as they departed on their onward flight from Dubai to New York. Their cheers illustrated their enthusiasm at having been chosen by Jansen for his F1 project, an adventure he hoped would give them the intellectual tools and emotional outlook to fulfil the promise of transformation begun with the end of apartheid a generation before.

Once in New York, the Kovsies split into small groups. Some stayed behind at New York University. Others headed off to various other institutions – Cornell, Cleveland State, Holy Cross, Mount Holyoke College, Appalachian State, the University of Minnesota, the University of Massachusetts, Binghamton, Amherst and the University of Washington. A dozen students went to Texas A&M University (also known as TAMU).

I betray my own prejudices when I say Texas A&M stood out when I reviewed the list of host campuses. Conservative Texas also has its counterpart to the sjambok-wielding stereotypical image of the Afrikaner: the cowboy-hatted redneck. For Americans, the term 'redneck' brings to mind enough images to fill a museum of stereotypes. A pickup truck and a mobile home would be essential exhibits. At its least judgmental, the term refers to a labourer – on a farm, on a road crew, on a construction site. His head is bowed at his task, exposing his neck to be reddened by the sun. This redneck is an honest worker, struggling by on a low wage, for whom sunburnt skin is a badge of honour. The word, however, is usually used as an insult. The redneck labourer is considered by some to be uneducated, unsophisticated, fearful of the unknown, racist and xenophobic to the point of violence.

I was not able to accompany the South African students to Texas, but I was eager to understand what they had experienced there. So, months after their programme had ended, and after they had emailed introductions on my behalf to friends they had made in the US, I went to Texas. My own journey taught me much about the capacity of some people from my own country to face history and commit themselves to building a better future. I also discovered ways in which Americans can learn from South Africans and I became aware of the confidence the Kovsies had gained from learning that when they spoke, their American peers listened.

Texas A&M is in the town of College Station, 140 kilometres north-west of Houston. It was founded in 1876 – around the same time that UFS has its origins. It was established with more or less the same objective as UFS, namely to help rural white communities educate themselves out of poverty and political marginalisation.

The first president of what would become Texas A&M, Thomas Gathright, was nominated by Jefferson Davis, who had led the Confederate States of America during the 1861–1865 American Civil War. The war that broke out over the south's determination to continue enslaving black Americans has been described by historian Shelby Foote as a 'revolution against change', doomed from its inception because of its flawed rationale.[42] Texas was among the first of the slaveholding states to break away from the Union.

TAMU was founded in the waning years of the post-Civil War period known as Reconstruction. American newspaperman W. J. Cash, an analyst of the southern American mind, quotes a letter sent to a newspaper that summed up the social and political upheaval in the south at the time. The letter also illustrated the impetus behind the founding of institutions like the college that would eventually become TAMU.

A decade after the war, the letter writer recounted seeing illiterate young whites being turned away from the polls because of laws limiting the franchise to those who could read and write. The writer states that his 'horse boy and other Negroes, taught by Northern teachers, were consistently admitted to the ballot. And I swore ... I should never cease from fighting for schools until every white child in the state had at least the surety of a common school education.'[43]

Two years after the main TAMU campus had opened, a branch of what was then known as the Agricultural and Mechanical College of Texas (hence A&M) was founded 'for the benefit of coloured youths' at Prairie View, 80 kilometres from College Station. Texas A&M's secondary black college was a 'separate but unequal institution,' acknowledges the university's historian, Henry C. Dethloff.[44]

Students there were relegated to learning the types of trades that the Texas lawmakers no doubt envisaged they would put to use as workers serving white employers: typesetting, printing, blacksmithing, carpentry, the basics of agriculture and teaching. Black students were not permitted to enrol at the main campus in College Station until the 1960s.

On the plane to Houston, there was more cheering from the South Africans. Eddie de Wet, a UFS psychology student from Vereeniging, remembers that the enthusiasm waned slightly, however, in the fierce heat they experienced on the drive to the TAMU campus at College Station.

Something brings Bloemfontein to mind when I look at College Station's sprawl of low-rise buildings, in hues that seem to fade into the landscape, or just beat the sun to its bleaching intentions. During my own visit there, I found myself wondering, in a moment of disorientation, why the street signs in Texas don't offer directions in English and in Afrikaans, as they do in the Free State. The preponderance of maroon and white, the college colours of TAMU, then quickly remind me that I'm not in Bloemfontein: I am in the home of the Aggies, as TAMU students are known. One College Station shop offers lacy little maroon dresses for Aggies planning a night on the town. Another sells artificial Christmas trees dyed maroon and white.

Any stranger who questioned the South Africans on that hot day of their arrival would have heard the whole story of why the students from UFS had landed in Aggie land. De Wet and his classmates, some of whom had never previously been out of South Africa, were being given a chance to see that the world was much bigger than they had imagined, but that they had a role to play in it. They would glimpse how higher education worked in other countries, and interact with strangers they could become friends with despite their different backgrounds, cultures and languages. And they would return, their university rector hoped, better equipped to change South Africa.

With his round, boyish face, alert green eyes, close-cropped blond hair and shirts that always seem slightly rumpled, De Wet looks like the head boy he was in high school. Before that, he had also been head boy at his primary school. And De Wet is, in a way, head boy of the group of South Africans who spent an intensive week and a half in Texas. He kept the group's electronic diary, his typos perhaps a result of exhaustion and excitement. When his mother knew he was about to arrive in Texas, she sent him an order via cellphone text: 'You won't sleep. Embrace every moment.' De Wet has saved that message, and claims that he slept only two hours a day when he was in America.

In the e-diary, he records that an 'early-bird group' had attended an 8 a.m. class on pluralism, stereotyping and prejudice: 'The lecture was given by A&M's first African American prof. And it was some motivation very applicable to our programme on not only tolerance, but finally celebrating diversity and being able to [live] in an open society, as more diversity equals better success.'

He quotes one of the TAMU professors, Alvin Larke (from the Department of Agricultural Leadership, Education and Communications), whom I later met, who said to the students: 'When people call you names that don't describe you [they're] not talking to you.'

The students attended classes on African history, religion in the Middle East and Arabs in America after the 9/11 terror attacks. There were late-night sessions, with the leaders of student groups tackling everything from race and gender discrimination to the lack of clean water in African villages. 'We had political stuff, cultural stuff, racial and gender-oriented stuff – everything,' De Wet recalls of the sessions at TAMU.

His was the first F1 group from UFS to have gone to TAMU, and they made a point of being on their best behaviour – accepting every invitation and making an effort to contribute to the classroom discussions. 'They wanted to impress us, and we wanted to impress them,' De Wet says.

The give and take of an American classroom is foreign to young South Africans who have spent their high-school years cramming for national exams in an education system that rewards rote memorisation, as opposed to an open exchange of ideas and ideals. Nevertheless, De Wet's group impressed the teachers at TAMU like Professor Larke, who says the South Africans brought pertinent questions to his class. Larke tells me that when he thinks back to the UFS students' visit, they didn't get as much from the TAMU students as the TAMU students got from them. 'I think that my students that semester gained so much respect for a different culture,' he says.

Larke, his eyes lively behind glasses, is a black professor on a predominantly white campus. He teaches young men and women who plan to go on to become teachers. Larke says many come from isolated rural communities where they rarely meet people who are not like them. Yet they have assumptions about those who are not middle class and white.

Larke makes the point that 'no literature exists that a poor person doesn't value education. No literature exists that a person of colour can't achieve. We have to transform the thoughts of individuals, young and old, about education. We've got to say education is for everyone, and everyone can succeed.'

So, even before they spoke in his class, the picture the South Africans presented was striking, Larke says. There they were: black and white, some wealthy and some struggling financially. Together.

Stephanie Curs, who teaches at the College of Agriculture and Life Sciences, notes the arcing symbolism the South Africans brought to TAMU. 'When they first got here, they were still pretty separated. The white students kind of stayed together,' she says. Then, she saw the South Africans beginning to make plans together, discussing how they could bring their collective experience of their study trip to the US back home to their fellow South Africans. Curs says she and others at TAMU were struck by the journey they saw the South Africans make. They started off in the kinds of racial groupings not uncommon on an American campus, but then they came together as a team in just a few days.

After the UFS students had left, she and her colleagues discussed how they could help replicate this kind of progress among their American students. 'The UFS students,' she says, 'and South Africans in general have been through so much more than most of our students can even fathom.'

Meanwhile, the South African students found that their American counterparts were very much aware of how far South Africa has come. It was as if, until foreigners pointed it out, the young South Africans had never realised that South Africa's peaceful transition from apartheid to democracy was an extraordinary effort of will and imagination.

Among the lectures they attended was Curs's class on global social-justice issues in agriculture. The class was created at the request of students who had been involved in projects to help the needy in and around College Station, and who wanted to expand that with a class that would study development and aid projects in other parts of the world. As part of the class, students have designed and executed international aid projects of their own. One year, students in the class sold mugs and T-shirts to raise a $3 000 donation for an international NGO that provides clean-water infrastructure in underdeveloped countries. In the classroom, students engage in role playing to understand the challenges facing families in the rural developing world. The students from America have never faced such difficulties in their own lives, 'but people around the world do – every day,' says Curs, who has worked in Asia helping impoverished women become entrepreneurs.

When the South Africans visited Curs's class, the topic turned to parallels between the South African anti-apartheid and US civil-rights movements. Curs noticed a certain hesitation in the South Africans. 'It's almost as if they felt ashamed of what South Africa had gone through,' she says. She told them: 'This is nothing to be ashamed of. You're the generation that's going to change this.'

'It has happened,' she told them. 'We can't go back and change it. But we can grow from it. And we can learn from it.'

Magon Mouton hails from Upington, a town known as one of the hottest places in South Africa, so she was not as perturbed by the Texan heat as her fellow Kovsie Eddie de Wet. However, in Curs's social-justice class, she found herself profoundly surprised by something else: the Americans approached events from South Africa's struggle against apartheid from a distance that gave them the perspective to draw lessons. Mouton hadn't realised how closely the world had watched events as they unfolded dramatically, a lifetime ago for her, in her own country. She explains how she had grown up knowing about the anti-apartheid struggle, and then she had studied it at school, where it was taught as part of history:

We actually grew up with it. But in America, it was different. I think sometimes we see it as in the past, something that just happened. In America, they studied it in depth: why did it happen? What led to the struggle? What happened afterwards? It makes it interesting for them to learn about this.

What may be interesting from a cool distance can be emotional and painful when the past is so recent. But Mouton could, likewise, look at American history with dispassion, and draw lessons.

'I feel like South Africa and America have a lot of similarities. They went through a struggle, with Martin Luther King and Jim Crow,' she says, referring to the iconic US civil-rights leader of the 1960s, and the post-Civil War legal restrictions on black Americans known as the Jim Crow System.

'Apartheid is very similar to aspects of American history,' she says. 'They are past it. Maybe we can do that [in South Africa] as well.'

For Mouton, the trip to America was her first real journey abroad. (Although she visits family in Namibia, that's her comfort zone, so it doesn't really count.) Now, she is considering postgraduate studies at TAMU. She wants more opportunities to learn about 'how other people experience different situations'.

Mashudu Ndwammbi, a classmate of Mouton, grew up with his Venda family in Thohoyandou, Limpopo. As a law student, he is aware that South Africa's Constitution explicitly bans unfair discrimination on the basis of race, gender, pregnancy, marital status, ethnic or social origin, colour, sexual orientation, age, disability, religion, conscience, belief, culture, language and birth. The Constitution enshrines a list of rights equally long, including the right to strike; to live in a healthy environment; and to have access to housing and healthcare, including reproductive healthcare, and sufficient food and water.

What Ndwammbi did not know before he visited the US was that legal experts around the world marvel at the depth and breadth of the charter that South Africans adopted in 1996, two years after apartheid had been brought to an end. Here, he displays gaps in his knowledge of his country's recent history, which I found to be not uncommon among the UFS students. I link the ignorance to a youthful determination to look ahead, as if even acknowledging the past by studying it would be to wallow in its most painful chapters. Within the F1 programme, it's almost as if the past sneaks up on students like a band of guerrillas, surprising the young South Africans before they can react.

Ndwammbi says he feels good that people know about South Africa, which he discovered after a conversation with an American about legal protections in South Africa. 'They know the good things, and not just Mandela. People know that we are moving forward. As a law student, that gave me a lot of pride in our Constitution.'

In De Wet's words, 'South Africa is on the map. We just don't know it here.' He admits that even if that were the only thing he learnt while in the US, it would be enough to make him happy. Seeing his country's past from a different perspective has made it clear that if one were to return to South Africa and do something important, the achievement would be recognised. He says the experience made the South Africans more proud of what they have.

A harmonic convergence of people and aspirations put TAMU among the institutions that have hosted UFS students participating in the F1 programme. Among the key people, I learn in College Station, is Eric Bost, who was the US ambassador to South Africa from 2006 until he was named TAMU's vice president for global initiatives in 2009.

Bost's role encompasses overseeing TAMU's formal research agreements with foreign institutions, its study-abroad programmes, its overseas campuses and its outreach activities to international students. In 2010 Bost led a fact-finding trip to Africa, which included a stop at UFS.

Alan Sams is the executive associate dean for TAMU's College of Agriculture and Life Sciences, and was part of that tour. He tells me his university actively seeks out partner institutions with similar missions and programmes that can expose the Texan students to new histories and heritages. Sams sees parallels between TAMU and UFS. One is historical. The Free State is the successor to what was briefly an independent Boer republic in the second half of the 19th century. Similarly, Texans declared their independence from Mexico in 1836; nine years later, the Republic of Texas was annexed to the United States.

More importantly, though, Sams sees something akin to what in the US are known as land-grant institutions in UFS's agriculture programmes and its commitment to helping South Africa overcome its economic challenges. These challenges include addressing rural poverty and the income gulf between the races left by apartheid.

Land-grant institutions are meant to make higher education accessible to more Americans and improve agriculture training across the country. Civil War-era President Abraham Lincoln signed the legislation creating them in 1862. The central ideology of the land-grant system is 'to serve the people's needs', explains Sams. 'It's the mission of this university to solve the needs of society.'

TAMU and other American institutions are facing the challenge of serving an increasingly diverse society. In May 2012, the US Census Bureau announced something new in the history of American demographics. Looking at births between July 2010 and July 2012, the statisticians found for the first time that babies of white European ancestry no longer formed the majority: 50.4 per cent of the population was made up of black, Hispanic or other non-white groups.[45]

Black students formed just over three per cent of TAMU's autumn 2012 enrolment of more than 50 000, and Hispanic students 16 per cent. However, when TAMU's students head out into the real world, it is one in which black Texans form 12 per cent of the state's population, and Hispanics 38 per cent. Sams believes that one of TAMU's challenges is to help its students learn and grow in a racially diverse environment. 'As many higher-education institutions in the States have learnt ... the educational experience for our students is enhanced through diversity,' he says.

During his first visit to UFS, he heard South Africans expressing similar concerns. And then he heard about the F1 programme. On the spot, Sams says, TAMU extended an invitation to host an F1 group. 'We thought that F1 complemented our needs and our mission and our priorities,' he says. 'It was bringing South Africa to Texas A&M and our classrooms.'

The South Africans set an example that provided 'a tremendous growth experience for our students,' Sams says. 'An example of how people of different races can have friendships like that is one that we don't see much here. It's good for our students to see that, to see those students getting along.'

The examples weren't limited to race, either. A colleague of Sams overheard a discussion about language among the South Africans. One was chiding another for speaking Afrikaans, saying that it left out non-Afrikaans speakers. English is unlikely to lose its place as the only official language in the US. Americans nonetheless debate, sometimes passionately, how and whether to accommodate those who speak other languages, including Spanish, which has deep roots in Texas and elsewhere in the US. While it's one thing for Americans to talk about Spanish versus English, the South Africans presented their American hosts with a real language question.

On visits to UFS, Sams has also been struck by the university administration's attempts to heal the divide between the different races, and by what he sees as parallels between his university's struggle to embrace diversity. In the US, he says, legislative and political decisions have ensured that all Americans are equal before the law. However, attitudes about race have lagged behind policy. 'We still struggle with that today,' Sams says.

He believes Americans and South Africans are on a similar journey, 'but we're about 20 years ahead'.

Other Americans who have visited UFS tell me that what they saw in South Africa reminds them of America as segregation waned and the proposition that all Americans were entitled to the same civil rights began to gain hard-fought ground in the 1960s.

In America, questions of race are now mostly fought out in legislatures and courtrooms. Some of the fiercest confrontations have been over education. The highest US court, the Supreme Court, has upheld the 'use of race as one of many "plus factors" in an admissions program that considered the overall individual contribution of each candidate'.

In 2008 a white candidate was refused admission to the University of Texas. She sued, claiming consideration of race in admissions violated all Americans' right to be treated and protected equally under the law. The case ended up in the Supreme Court, which issued a decision in 2013 that universities across the US read very closely. The court decided that judges are required to give any university substantial leeway 'both in the definition of the compelling interest in diversity's benefits and in deciding whether its specific plan was narrowly tailored to achieve its stated goal'.

In its decision on the 2008 University of Texas suit, the Supreme Court did not rule that universities could not consider race when making admissions decisions, but did rule that universities must be very careful when making racial considerations.

In terms of race relations on campus, TAMU has made progress, if at times fitfully, since its founding in 1876. In 2001, an exhibition at the university's archives set out to capture the history of race relations at the university. At the time, the exhibit's curator told *The Bryan-College Eagle*, the local daily newspaper, that little had been compiled before he started poring over clippings, photographs and letters, and conducting interviews.

He told *The Eagle*, 'You realise that there are a lot of frustrations, but there's also a lot to celebrate. For any Southern university, A&M's history is no different. One person explained to me A&M opened the door for African Americans, they just didn't put a welcome mat down.'

Reading through material in the archives gave me an insight into TAMU's history. I also got a chance to see the past through the eyes of men who had lived it themselves when I met with former students Hugh McElroy, James Thomas Reynolds and Samuel Williams.

In the early 1960s, McElroy was among the first black students at Texas A&M. It took protests, legal challenges and national legislation to change once all-white institutions like TAMU across the US. The campaign culminated in January

1964, when the US Congress passed the Civil Rights Act, which included the provision that 'no person in the United States shall, on the ground of race, colour or national origin, be excluded from participation in, be denied the benefits of, or be subjected to discrimination under any program or activity receiving federal financial assistance'.

I met McElroy in his office at his alma mater, where he is now director for institutional advancement at the School of Rural Public Health. His office decor includes a football and a battered helmet. McElroy played football, the sport at the centre of campus life, for A&M at a time when the team coach expressed reservations that having a black player would damage team unity. That McElroy was able to earn fame as a player is proof of the commitment of the university president at the time, James Earl Rudder, who had declared that everyone, regardless of their race, would have an opportunity on his campus.

By 1964, Rudder, a high-school and college football coach, and World War II hero, had served as TAMU's president for four years and would serve for another six, until his death in 1970. His letters from the time, preserved in the university archives, paint a portrait of a man who eschewed drama and with soldierly determination set out to complete the mission he had been given to open the university to all races.

In his own way, McElroy had to learn the language to navigate different worlds. He was raised by his grandmother, who worked as a maid in white households in Houston. He recounts how one potential employer asked whether she had a health certificate confirming she didn't have any diseases she might pass on to the family.

'She said, "Yes, I do. But do *you* have one? Because I'm going to be cleaning *your* toilets",' McElroy tells me. 'And that was the way she presented herself. She was going to stand up for herself. She did not have a sense of subservience. She had a sense of right and wrong. And she instilled that in me.'

McElroy sat me down at the conference table in his office and arranged a call with James Thomas Reynolds and Samuel Williams. The three had been friends since their student days. Williams had arrived in 1964 not only as one of the first black TAMU students, but also as one of the first black members of the Corps of Cadets, a tradition-bound military organisation that had been part of the university since its beginnings.

Shortly before he arrived to start classes, Williams had been told he'd be sharing an apartment with two black cadets instead of living in a corps dormitory. University President Rudder stepped in to veto the separate housing plan, Williams tells me, quoting Rudder as saying, 'If we're going to do this, we're going to do it right. They're going to be in the Corps, like anybody else.' Williams was assigned to a corps outfit, in a dormitory.

Reynolds, who also was a cadet, says they were serious about what they were trying to achieve during their years in College Station. 'We were students. We were trying to make grades and get a degree and move on,' he says. 'Because we were not out there, loud and boisterous and starting things, I do believe it helped to defuse a lot of things.'

They learned when to show restraint, such as the time a cross was burned outside McElroy's dormitory room. That kind of anonymous threat leaves little scope for retaliation. At whom do you strike back?

Other occasions, though, called for action. Reynolds recalls facing hostility from a white student one evening in the dining hall. The student stared at him, then went further: 'He called me some interesting names.' Reynolds showed restraint in the hall. 'You just don't smack somebody there with all these people watching. I surely wanted to.'

The white student didn't let it go, and approached him later, outside the hall: 'I don't think this guy really wanted to fight. After I slapped him, he just looked at me and that was it. We walked away.'

A friend and room-mate of Reynolds, who was white, had been nearby during the incident, ready to intervene on his behalf, Reynolds said. 'He was a different kind of cat,' Reynolds said fondly of the room-mate, who has remained a friend. Reynolds says,

> He and I had all kinds of discussions about black and white culture. I must say, I was pretty fortunate to have a fellow of the opposite race who was unlike what was going on in the South. It didn't surprise me that there were people like that, because, growing up in the South, with your parents mixing in and involved with people, you have a chance to associate and have contact with individuals of the white race who were different.

Inspired by discussions with his room-mate, Reynolds developed a kind of do-it-yourself multicultural-awareness class, foreshadowing some of the strategies university officials around the world today are devising to prepare their students for a diverse world. Says Reynolds:

> Somebody might say, 'You're a coloured boy.' I would say, 'Well, what colour am I?' It's interesting how those kind of comments could open up conversations. I would seek out dialogues with individuals, just to get into their heads and try to understand what was making them tick. I did my own personal study of what was going on – why should someone dislike me who doesn't even know who I am? I wanted to know why would someone hate me, when, in fact, I should be hating *them*.
>
> After so many hours of asking questions of white friends or individuals I didn't know too well, it opened up the door for them to ask me questions.

Reynolds got a degree in wildlife science at A&M, which prepared him to realise a long-held dream of working as a national park ranger.

Williams's degree in engineering led to a career at General Electric before he launched his own business.

McElroy left TAMU with a degree in industrial technology and has worked in the corporate and academic worlds. He's proud of having worked for employers like Exxon, and proud of work he sees as helping to build a university for all. His current job at his old university is his second there: in the 1990s, he served the university as associate director of human resources.

A day or so after my talk with McElroy and the classmates of his era, I met a black student currently studying at TAMU, Mikeala Carter, who comes from a suburb of the Texas metropolis of Dallas. It's disturbing, but not particularly surprising, to hear her first-hand account of how prejudice has persisted on campus.

'A lot of times, on the news, they talk about how we're in a post-racial society. Then I'm with my friends here, and one of them gets called a nigger. It is disturbing to know that I'm having the same experience that someone had 50 years ago,' says Carter.

Most of Carter's classmates at her high school in Dallas were like her: black and middle class. However, at TAMU it is not unusual for her to find she is the only black student in class. 'My mom always told me the world isn't going to be like your high school,' she says. And she has come to embrace her years at TAMU as an opportunity to learn how to get along in a wider world, even if it sometimes can be tough.

Carter arrived at TAMU in 2007, a historic moment in the US, the eve of the election of Barak Obama, the son of a white mother and a black father, to the presidency. On campus, Carter found, to her horror, that white students were selling T-shirts with one of the school's football slogans given a presidential theme: 'Beat the hell out of Obama.' Days before the elections, a conservative student group encouraged people to throw eggs at a poster of Obama.

Carter did not think this was just about politics. TAMU is considered Republican country and Obama is from the rival Democratic Party, but respect for authority also is deeply ingrained. 'I think a lot of it was about race,' Carter says, questioning whether a white Democrat would have been subjected to similar abuse. 'I just thought it was very disrespectful, regardless of who the candidate was.'

While she believes some white students harbour racist views, Carter admits she's also seen friendships across the colour divide. 'You do see a lot of camaraderie between different people,' she says. 'You have to love all people,' she says. 'But you don't have to accept bigoted attitudes toward you.'

In South Africa, the Reitz video would spark change at UFS. In 2006 TAMU also had a scandal over racism involving a video and the Internet. *The Battalion*, the student newspaper, reported that a video produced by TAMU students had 'depicted a student with shoe polish on his face, acting as a slave caught using his "master's" Internet. The "master" then proceeded to whip and abuse the student. An alternative ending showed the "master" sodomising the "slave".'

The university president at the time called the video 'hateful'. Three students involved in producing and distributing it on the Internet withdrew from the college. One of the three videographers explained in a letter to *The Battalion*, which had called the video 'fiercely anti-Aggie', that it had been made two years earlier, when the three were freshmen, in an attempt to call attention to racism on campus through satire. The letter writer said that once the three had viewed the 'exercise in our home movie-making skills', they agreed it was too clumsy to serve their purpose and should be destroyed. But one failed to destroy his copy and it was – apparently mistakenly – uploaded onto YouTube.

'As a participant who showed very poor personal judgment in being involved with this video in the first place, my apologies to all who have been hurt and offended,' the videographer wrote, signing himself as 'One Sorry ex-Aggie'.[46]

The 'Sorry ex-Aggie' claims that he is no racist, but that he understands the video that he had tried to hide would be perceived as racist.

Like American society in general, TAMU has struggled and sometimes stumbled, but it has also changed in ways that might astound the first black students who enrolled there back in the 1960s. Black students have led the student council and the university's Corps of Cadets; black administrators and professors have been appointed. One of them is Professor Larke, who arrived in College Station to teach in 1984, after earning a doctorate in agricultural education at the University of Missouri.

A specialist in diversity in higher education, Larke knew he would have to transform some thinking on a less-than-diverse campus. But first, he tells me, he had to transform himself. His story is one that I believe will resonate with South Africans, not because of any parallels when it comes to issues of race and history, but because of the personal choices made that speak to universal values.

Larke grew up in an era when a black man from the southern states intent on getting an education could face violence from racist whites. He says he experienced some of the treatment that is still in the forefront of Americans' minds when they recall the civil-rights movement, when white law-enforcement officers would use fire-engine hoses as water cannons against protesters, or unleash attack dogs on demonstrators. Nevertheless, Larke got his undergraduate and master's degrees at South Carolina State College, which used to be an institution for black students only, and which is now South Carolina State University. He went north, to the University of Missouri, to study for his doctorate in agricultural education.

Returning south to a historically white university meant he 'had to rethink whites', he says. He told himself that his new colleagues in Texas were 'not the people who sprayed me with water. They are not the people who denied me free access to education.'

In 1996, two years after apartheid had ended in South Africa, Larke became the first black educator to be named a full professor at TAMU. While his colleagues congratulated him, he contemplated why it had taken so long. He found the answer in the attitudes of black as well as white Americans.

Larke says that his father had been baffled that his son wanted to go to college, instead of taking on a role the elder Larke was more confident would be available to a black American high-school leaver: going to work, or joining the military. To see his son pursue a doctorate, and then teach at what he saw as a 'white school' was even more baffling. The son, however, sees TAMU as a school for everyone.

A few years before he became professor, Larke had been invited to speak at a rural high school near College Station during Black History Month. (Since the 1970s, American presidents have designated February as the month to honour the contributions African Americans have made to the country, and the month is often marked with speeches by prominent African Americans at schools and libraries.) Larke was so impressed by the poise of the black teenager who introduced him at the event that afterwards he asked the boy's teachers whether he might be interested in attending TAMU. The teachers, who were white, told Larke they didn't think the young man was TAMU material because he came from a broken home. A career counsellor, who was also white, said the young man should not aspire to anything higher than a technical college.

Larke decided to wait in the school library until classes were over so he could speak to the young man himself. He says he asked him, 'If I got you a scholarship to come to A&M, would you come?'

He went home with the young man that evening, so that he could speak to his mother and grandparents. Larke says the mother had little to say, but the grandfather showed an interest, even though other black Texans in the community were sceptical that one of their own would be welcome at TAMU.

The young man enrolled at TAMU in 1991. He didn't leave until he had completed his doctorate in 2000. Larke mentored him over the years, and advised him to hold a celebration for achieving his doctorate at his own home, so he could be an example to other young black people in his community.

Larke was left wondering how many other black potential students had been discouraged by their elders. It was his white teachers who had told the young man that he wasn't qualified to go to university, Larke says. And it was black neighbours who had told him no one from their community had ever gone to TAMU.

Back in the Free State, Jonathan Jansen foresees UFS students becoming more diverse, and racial issues becoming less heated. But he does not foresee a diminishing need for students to travel overseas and broaden their thinking, and remain in touch with the larger world.

'I always want them to think of the world as interconnected, interrelated,' he tells me. 'And that the struggles of, say, Texas A&M, are not dissimilar in terms of racism, slavery, oppression. And, then, hope.'

The F1 leadership programme strives to teach students exactly this.

6. Unexpected encounters

t is a late-summer morning in 1996. I'm waiting for a bright-eyed 10-year-old to get ready for school. Her parents are among a group of black South Africans who had filed a lawsuit to force a government school in Potgietersrus (now Mokopane) to drop admissions policies designed to keep black students out. My plan is to report on the day in part through the eyes of this family.

We reach school to find a crowd of white protesters railing against the policy that compels their children to be educated alongside black children. It will lead to them losing their culture, they claim. One protester shouts in Afrikaans that the black students are 'apes'. I am both frightened and saddened by the protesters, who seem capable of anything in their panic, yet vulnerable in their confusion, and I am relieved to find a police presence at the school.

I wonder how that day shaped those children, black and white, who are young adults now. How many of the black students would grow up unable to see whites as anything but violent and selfish? How many of the white students, drawing cues from parents they trusted, would never be able to see eye to eye with a fellow South African who was black?

Despite this, I also saw reason for hope that day. I joked with colleagues that the 10-year-old we accompanied to school was so vivacious that white students would soon be clamouring to be her friend.

By the second day, the crowds of protesters had dwindled. An eight-year-old white student, who had been kept home the day before, told reporters that she was now at school to show the black children around. 'I want to help them, because they're new,' she said, and with those words, she transformed a moment of crisis into an ordinary morning in class.

The stereotypes that have defined race relations in South Africa are powerful, and have been fuelled over the decades by confrontations like the one I witnessed in Potgietersrus. But the fresh energy and perspective the young can bring to the discussion are also powerful in breaking down those barriers and prejudices.

On my mission in Texas to learn more about the South African students' experiences in the US and the impact they made, I made a point of seeking out Danielle Harris, vice dean of TAMU's College of Agriculture and Life Sciences, because Harris designed the agenda for the visiting Kovsies. It was a task she took on in addition to her regular duties, which include recruiting and mentoring new students.

Harris, an African American, is committed to making students of all races and backgrounds feel welcome on her campus. Amid the decor of her office, I glimpse a memento from another time, a black-and-white photo with the caption 'coloured school room – 1945'. It also bears a motto: 'Being able to see past traditional barriers and having an intense belief in your ideas and abilities will help you take advantage of any opportunity.'

Harris put together a class schedule for the South Africans, and arranged trips for them to the state fair and a rodeo hall. The core part of her agenda – hosting the UFS visitors in the homes of TAMU students' families – almost failed to happen because of concerns about logistics and liability.

In the end, those who hosted and those who were hosted say the personal time they spent together as a result was among the most memorable aspects of the trip, and led to long-term friendships. The young people, when free of professorial supervision, spent evenings together at cafes and clubs. The South Africans tagged along to meetings of the student organisations to which their American hosts belonged. The Americans took their guests to a football game, which Harris had not included in the official schedule.

Jessica Guerra, a Texan studying international relations and business, took Lara Brown, a South African studying occupational therapy, into her home in College Station. 'Half of everything we said was questions,' Guerra remembers from the time she spent with the UFS students. 'They were so curious, and so ready to learn.'

In addition to the heart-to-heart talks, there was an evening laid on for the visitors featuring an A&M choir: 'We all had goosebumps when they started singing "Nkosi Sikelel'iAfrika",' group leader Eddie de Wet wrote in his diary.

De Wet was just as moved by a monthly memorial service

held in honour of A&M students who have died. He says the ritual evoked a sense of family and unity he would like to see at UFS.

He was also fascinated by A&M's '12th man' tradition – the idea that you don't have to be among the 11 players on a football team to make a contribution, that no one is on the sidelines. Harris sent each of the Kovsies home with one of the white towels embroidered with the words '12th man' in maroon, which Aggies wave during football games. As she distributed the towels, Harris told the South Africans there would be days ahead when things weren't going right. She wanted them to remember the best of their days in Texas to help them raise their spirits when they were feeling down.

De Wet spent over four hours on his feet – as a venerable A&M tradition demands – at a football game under the huge dome of the Dallas Cowboys Stadium, where the Aggies played the Arkansas Razorbacks. Standing throughout a game is an A&M tradition that goes back to 1922, when a team from College Station played one of the first post-season championships, known as a bowl game, against Centre College in Dallas. A reserve player, considered so unlikely to be called on for the Aggies that he wasn't even dressed in his football gear, was spending the game in the press box. When injuries decimated his team's substitutes, however, the coach brought on the reserve player and made him kit up in the injured captain's team outfit.

'Legend says his readiness spurred the Aggies to the upset 22-14 victory,' writes Dethloff. Students 'soon adopted the custom, now a hallowed tradition, of standing for all football games, signifying their readiness to be the 12th Man'.[47]

At the Dallas game, De Wet watched his hosts' side lead until the last five minutes, but they lost at the final whistle. Nevertheless, he marvelled at the team spirit, even if he found the action on the field lame compared with rugby.

De Wet was also impressed by a project that Aggies his age had organised. They had established a car pool – a network of weekend, on-call drivers who drive rented cars and are linked by mobile phones and computers, ready to ferry fellow students too drunk to get themselves home safely from parties. De Wet wants to bring the same idea to UFS, and not just for party-goers, but also for poor students who have to get to homes in faraway townships after classes. Laws may no longer confine black South Africans to townships, but the legacy of lifetime after lifetime of inequality has left most black South Africans too poor to live anywhere else.

'If you study until late at night and you have to get a taxi home, the car pool would love to be the person taking you home, being responsible for you and knowing that you're safe,' he says.

He met another group of Americans encouraging fellow students to drink only tap water for 10 days. They then donate the money they might otherwise have spent on soft drinks to a development group that digs wells in Africa.

These resourceful groups, he says, showed him that leadership was about looking beyond yourself and narrow definitions of identity – not only thinking about your campus, but also society and the community as a whole.

The learning experience went in both directions, however, and sometimes in surprising ways. During her search for hosts for the UFS students, Harris came into contact with a South African who had made it to College Station off his own bat. Warren Chalklen had come to TAMU earlier that year for postgraduate studies after having studied Zulu and English at the University of the Witwatersrand in his home town. As part of his teacher training at Wits, he had taught in rural schools in South Africa, an experience that gave Chalklen, who is white and from a privileged background, a close look at the lives of South Africa's impoverished black majority, and what he calls the 'deep, structural remnants of apartheid'.

'As white South Africans, there's a tendency to deny our place in the country,' he says. 'I've taken a conscious decision to be part of the new South Africa.'

He is studying for a doctorate in public administration in Texas and plans to return to South Africa to work in government to help shape education policy, doing what he can to close the gap he witnessed as a student teacher. Apartheid, he says, has yet to be completely dismantled.

'South Africans need quality education,' Chalklen argues. 'We cannot transform the country without excellence, without the human capital.'

Working with TAMU's Center for Urban School Partnerships, he observed some of the impact on American schools of poverty, inequality and neglect. He has volunteered for a TAMU campus group whose aim is to raise awareness about gay, lesbian, bisexual and transgender students – people who might well feel ostracised on a conservative campus. He has reached out to other international students. In a sense, he is studying how outsiders navigate TAMU.

African Americans he met before coming to Texas had told him to expect to find conservative, even racist, white students on a campus that was predominantly white. Chalklen says he was intrigued by what he saw as a chance to sample what South Africa had been like for his parents, though not on the scale or to the degree of apartheid.

And at TAMU, he would for the first time be living as part of a racial majority, and by experiencing race from that perspective, could get a new angle on the experiences of his parents, and perhaps learn new ways to talk to them about the changes he wants for their country.

Chalklen tells me: 'I am confronting my whiteness in the United States in a way that I've never confronted it before. Generations older than me, including my parents, participated actively in apartheid. Their children now are actively trying to dismantle what they did.'

According to him, this has created intergenerational tensions in South Africa. Chalklen includes himself when he describes the impact of apartheid: 'We were traumatised by this experience. We're still traumatised as a people in South Africa.'

In America, he says, he had listened to 'unemotional' discussions about race and racism. 'That's not the way we talk about things.'

Chalklen also found that Americans were quick to stereotype him as a white South African, and he chafed at being put into a box labelled 'racist' and 'aggrieved'. Yet, he too, could slip into making easy assumptions. Chalklen has caught himself treating cleaning staff at TAMU, workers who are often Hispanic, with the same easy disregard with which his parents might have treated black South African domestic workers or gardeners.

Then, fellow South Africans came to visit Chalklen's college, and the young man who had come to America to learn how to transform South Africa was given the gift of a new perspective on himself. He learnt that he too could be guilty of failing to go beyond unthinking assumptions. He learnt that he was also not without prejudice. But also not without the courage to transform.

When Harris told Chalklen that the UFS students were coming, he thought immediately of the major event in the recent history of the Bloemfontein university that had made news across South Africa and beyond – the Reitz video incident. Chalklen was still a student at Wits when he had watched the video for the first time. He heard it argued that the short clip was not representative of South African thinking a generation after apartheid's end. He was not so sure, however, and felt it was possible that Wits students could have been capable of making a similar video.

'What UFS has done, especially with Reitz, is hold the mirror to South Africa, and make us face the truth about what is happening in South Africa on a daily basis,' Chalklen says. The video, he says, 'appealed to the racism in everyone. It appealed to the patriarch in everyone; it appealed to the elitist in everyone – because everyone identified something of themselves in this one video, whether they were the oppressed or the oppressor. It's a reflection of the conversations that we are afraid to have.'

Chalklen had bristled during his early days in Texas when Americans assumed that because he was a white South African, he would think like a colonial white African:

> I was expected to think South Africa was going to go up in flames because of black rule. There was the expectation that I would participate in the bashing of Africa, and particularly the bashing of South Africa. And when I did not participate in that, I was often met with a flippant 'what do you know?' attitude.

So what did Chalklen do when he spoke to other prospective hosts in Texas about the South Africans whom they were contemplating welcoming into their homes? He told the Americans they might find deep-rooted prejudice among white South Africans – the very type of prejudice he had been trying to dissociate himself from. Some would try to play down the meaning of the Reitz video, he told the American students.

His first reaction was that he wanted to debrief the hosts,

Chalklen remembers when he was asked to join the group of hosts, many of whom were friends he had made among liberal and progressive thinkers at TAMU. 'I went to see the hosts and warned them about the people that they would be hosting. I think that the right word is "sensitise" – sensitise them to the people that they would be bringing into their homes.'

He gave the American students a warning:

> My whole thing was giving them a history of Reitz, talking to them frankly about Reitz, and about the fact that some of these students coming may really think that Reitz was fantastically funny and great. I said, 'You're going to have the white students come in and tell you, "South Africa is going to the dogs and I can't wait to get out."'

By 'white', Chalklen came to realise, he meant Afrikaners. Chalklen is a third-generation South African of English descent. He not only went to Wits, a leading English-speaking university, but to King Edward VII, an elite Johannesburg all-boys high school with stately buildings and a curriculum reminiscent of an English public school.

When the visitors arrived, however, Chalklen found none of the racism he had expected from Afrikaner students. Looking back, he now concedes that his dire predictions were a manifestation of 'my own perception of the University of the Free State, and my own prejudices that I have to acknowledge and own.'

The experience revealed his own demons. 'I'm trying to navigate everyone else's space. But I'm not navigating my own too well. That was an interesting journey,' he says of his time with the visitors from home. Then, as if underlining his words, he repeats them slowly: 'That was an interesting journey.'

During the Kovsies' visit, Chalklen was paired with Mias Nortier, a young Afrikaner studying to be a church minister. Chalklen, who prides himself on speaking several of South Africa's official languages, found that his Afrikaans was not up to the task of communicating in Nortier's first language. They made do with English and a smattering of Sotho, one of the languages of the black communities in the Bloemfontein area.

Before his trip to the US, Nortier had never been out of South Africa, except to visit a game park in neighbouring Botswana. And the landscape in Botswana, he says, was so much like what he was used to at home that he barely noticed he had crossed a border.

Texas may also have looked a lot like home. However, Nortier, who wears the universal student uniform of jeans and T-shirts along with mod, slightly tinted glasses and a spiky, boy-band haircut, found a lot to shake him during his two weeks at TAMU. At first, he was shocked to find the university had no theology school and intrigued by Americans' secular outlook. His university traces its history to a theological institution, and has only recently begun to tone down official references to Christianity as it tries to welcome students and staff of other faiths.

The UFS motto used to be '*In Deo Sapiente Lux*' ('In God is the light of wisdom'). It is now '*In Veritate Sapiente Lux*' ('In truth is the light of wisdom'). Nortier quotes Jonathan Jansen as saying that the university 'mustn't be a church'.

'I agree in certain ways,' Nortier says. And although it can be hard to process all the changes, 'you cannot be too narrow-minded these days,' he admits.

Nortier grew up in small-town Bultfontein, just 100 kilometres from Bloemfontein. After high school, he went to study to be a chef at a college in George, where English is more commonly spoken than Afrikaans. Until then, all his education had been at Afrikaans-only schools, so he had to work on his English and learn how to get along with non-Afrikaners both at chef school and during his first job in a hotel kitchen.

'In the rural areas, in the small towns, they don't love English,' he says, tracing the hostility to the language to memories and tales from when the Afrikaners were defeated by British imperial forces.

'There's this whole stigma about English, because they saw the British people as a threat, way back then – because of the Anglo-Boer War,' Nortier says. He says there is a whole misconception about English as a language.

Nortier worked as a chef for just six months: he found the work too hard, he jokes. Spurred on by a desire to serve the community in some way, which he still struggles to articulate, he decided to return to college, to train to be a teacher. Weeks before the classes started, he learnt that his home-town church could offer him a scholarship if he studied theology. He took this as a spiritual sign and switched career paths.

Nortier had grown up in a religious family, he says, but until then he had never considered becoming a preacher. And he had distanced himself from what many saw as the church of apartheid. A sense that the Church, too, is now trying to change was one of the things that drew him to study theology. He is studying at a university that is evolving, preparing to devote himself to a new type of Church and a new South Africa.

Nortier describes the continuing debate over the Belhar Confession, which was written in the 1980s by leaders of the churches specially established for black, Indian and coloured South Africans within the Dutch Reformed Church family. The Dutch Reformed Church (a white institution) denounced the document, which rejects segregation, claiming it had a political rather than a religious agenda. Today it is still a point of contention within the church.

The Belhar Confession was first adopted as an article of faith by increasingly assertive Dutch Reformed member churches whose congregations were not Afrikaner, and who are part of the Uniting Reformed Church in Southern Africa (which was formed the year apartheid ended by the merger of Dutch Reformed mixed-race and black congregations).

Slowly and fitfully, Afrikaners within the still separate Dutch Reformed Church in South Africa are embracing Belhar as they have embraced the end of a segregated church.

According to Nortier, leaders of his church 'are trying very hard to change now. The teachers tell us that we have to try to change. I see it as a challenge for our generation.'

When he visits his church at home in Bultfontein, Nortier finds the preacher in traditional black robes and there is only the organ to accompany the hymns. The church Nortier attends more regularly in Bloemfontein, however, has a full band with a light rock sensibility. The Bloemfontein preacher wears jeans and a T-shirt.

'You can see they're almost completely different worlds, even though they are only 100 kilometres apart,' Nortier says.

Nortier ended up travelling across an ocean to another continent to find that some of the answers he was seeking were to be found back home. Americans 'are actually struggling more than us,' he tells me. 'There, the white people are the majority. They can just ignore the others if they want. We can't.'

What he observed in the US – and perhaps encouraged by the example of the multilingual Chalklen – led Nortier to take up Sotho, the home language of many of his classmates at UFS. He started studying the language once he returned to his own campus after the trip to Texas. Nortier says that before visiting Texas, when he strolled across campus he often used to greet only fellow white South Africans. Many black students are from cultures where the exchange of greetings is a crucial courtesy. (A literal translation of the Zulu for 'hello' is 'I see you' – an acknowledgment of shared humanness.) The black students who Nortier failed to greet may have felt he was displaying rudeness or lack of understanding. Or just plain racism.

But Nortier says he simply feared that his Afrikaans greeting would have been read as an attempt to impose his language. He was uncertain of his English, and even more uncertain that fellow South Africans who were black would want to engage with an Afrikaans-speaker.

Now he's testing his Sotho 'hellos' and 'how are yous' on black students. His class load is heavy, with Greek and Hebrew required languages for theology, not Sotho and, some days, he thinks, 'Agh, why am I doing this? I don't have time.'

Then Nortier remembers why he applied to go to Texas in the first place, something else for which he had little time. It wasn't just the chance to go to America. 'We're 20 years after apartheid. But sometimes, it doesn't seem like that. I wanted to make my change.'

Since returning from Texas, Nortier has become convinced that his university should abandon offering classes in Afrikaans and English in favour of teaching only in English. That would bring black and white students together on a campus that is now, practically speaking, divided in two – with Afrikaans classes for whites and English classes for blacks. If teaching were offered only in English, it would force students across the racial divide to be with one another, Nortier believes.

But Nortier doesn't share this theory with fellow Afrikaners, who can be fiercely protective of their language. He prefers, he says, to lead by example. South Africans are too prone to preach at each other, he says: 'Everyone thinks they're right.'

Nortier describes an evening at home in Bultfontein with his family: 'When the news is on and President Zuma's there, they say, "Agh, not this man again!"'

The ANC has pledged to uplift South Africa's black and poor majority, and take them out of the poverty and ignorance created in large part by the deliberate inequalities of apartheid. Some white South Africans fear black South Africans will gain at their expense. Nortier has heard people in his home town complain that Afrikaners are losing ground in post-apartheid South Africa, saying things such as how difficult it is to be a white person now.

Like the Afrikaners he knew when he was growing up, Nortier questions whether government affirmative-action policies are being implemented fairly, and whether his generation of white South Africans are being made to pay for the mistakes of their forefathers. But he also believes that white South Africans in the past gained privileges at the cost of others, and that some action is needed to address that history.

'Now, we're no longer privileged. You have to work harder to get what you want. You must work to prove yourself,' he says.

As a minister, Nortier might be based in Bultfontein or some other small town like it. He says he would embrace the challenge and try to change mindsets.

He has already had a profound influence on the mindset of at least one person – fellow South African Warren Chalklen. If Chalklen had been paired during the F1 programme with a black South African, he might have brushed up on his Zulu and emerged from the experience satisfied with his own liberal credentials. Instead, he got to spend time with an Afrikaner student. When he discovered that Mias Nortier did not fit the stereotype of an Afrikaner, Chalklen was forced to confront the reality of his own prejudices about Afrikaners.

As Nortier and Chalklen jog together one evening in Texas, the future church minister from small-town South Africa mentions to the future educationist from South Africa's biggest city that he plans to have a braai when he returns to Bloemfontein. On the guest list will be all those who accompanied him to America. Nortier has to stop running for a moment to contemplate the idea that socialising across the colour line is now a matter of course.

'It was a powerful moment for me,' Chalklen says. 'That's when I realised the power of this thing, that we needed to take this group of young South Africans outside of South Africa, force them into one another's space and to have the conversation that they would never otherwise have had.'

Chalklen says that he saw among the UFS visitors to Texas 'the courage to at least begin'. And they helped him make a new beginning of his own.

'It was so good that they put me with Mias,' Chalklen says. 'He changed my life. He really did.'

7. Family matters

ddie de Wet has a dream of being a plastic surgeon one day. With his warm, back-slapping charm, it's easy to imagine him sketching out a facelift for a patient he's met on the golf course. But De Wet imagines himself reconstructing the faces and lives of accident victims. He is no country-club boy – even if he does occasionally play golf.

A UFS administrator says that, at first glance, De Wet seems like 'almost the stereotypical leader of a white male residence' – on the surface, the kind of rugby-mad South African one might expect to hear confessing casual racism in a bar. But in reality he's nothing like that. I saw how easy it would be to put someone like De Wet into a box marked 'typical Afrikaner', and I wanted to see what I could learn by digging deeper. I found a complicated character from a complicated background. De Wet's personal history gave him the capacity to defy stereotypes. His is an inspiring story.

De Wet's mother, Lizelle Oosthuizen, tells me he's always been a leader, a doer. He decided when he was in primary school that he wanted to be a doctor when he grew up. He did not make it into the well-regarded medical school at UFS when he applied in high school. So instead he enrolled to study genetics, then switched to psychology. While in Texas during the

F1 programme, De Wet devised a plan B: he may one day study medicine in the US.

His home town, Vereeniging, is an hour's drive south of Johannesburg, through a series of smaller towns with main streets named after the Voortrekkers. In each suburban centre, the spire of a Dutch Reformed church towers over the flat landscape.

The first sign of Vereeniging is the cooling towers of its electricity plant. Later, dull black hills can be glimpsed from the road, the debris discharged from coal mines.

Vereeniging has a golf course surrounded by gracious homes set in leafy gardens. However, De Wet grew up far from that neighbourhood, in the gritty town centre. Driving past the building where they lived in their first apartment, his mother shakes her head at the weeds now growing in the front yard and points out the balcony where her two boys once played. Nearby, the building that once housed the crèche that De Wet attended as a toddler also looks dilapidated.

He was shy when he started school. A photo from his crèche days shows him as a solemn little boy. But in photos after that, the young De Wet is smiling, showing early signs of the outgoing personality that he developed. At TAMU and later, back at UFS, when university staff had messages for students in his group, they turned to De Wet to disseminate them. When his classmates want to make a point to the administration, they deputise De Wet to speak on their behalf. He's the one who sends out email and Facebook reminders that his fellow Kovsies or Aggies have meetings to attend, or fund-raisers to plan. He organises the group Skype chats that bring together the Texan and South African students, who say they became friends for life during the Kovsies' visit to College Station.

As unprepossessing as it seems today, De Wet's home town has had its share of the world's attention. In May 1902, the generals and commanders who had led the Boer guerrilla fighters against the British in the Anglo-Boer War gathered in Vereeniging, then a frontier town, to debate whether it was time to surrender. They had little choice, given that big parts of the former Boer republics had been destroyed as part of the British Empire's scorched-earth policy, and their food and ammunition were running low together with the declining will to continue the fight.

Among those who put aside their pride to agree to the Peace of Vereeniging was another De Wet, General Christiaan de Wet, the famed guerrilla leader of the Orange Free State. De Wet, who remained fiercely republican, would lead the short-lived 1914 rebellion against the pro-British Union government when it opted to support Britain's efforts in the Great War.

Eddie de Wet doesn't know if he's related to the famous general, but he does know that De Wet is considered a hero among Afrikaners. He is fuzzy on the details, though. Many years have elapsed since he studied history at junior school, and when he got to high school, he says, he found that South African history was not emphasised. De Wet questions whether this was because of the politics of the time, just a decade after the end of apartheid.

'How do you choose what history people need to know?' De Wet asks. Today, he says, 'history sometimes makes things crazy'.

Frederick Fourie, rector of UFS in the period before De Wet enrolled, is an economist by training and a historian by inclination – and perhaps necessity. Yet he understands De Wet's reluctance to delve into history. That is youth's prerogative, Fourie believes: 'You're still climbing the mountain, looking up the slope. You have not stopped to look back.' Fourie also recognises that 'history can make you a prisoner'.

Fourie once co-taught a university course aimed at instilling in young people a sense of the possibility of history. It aimed to help them see that similar clashes arise again and again, but that new ways of resolving them can be found and to point out the parallels between the hopes of black South Africans living in shacks and the Afrikaners' determination to rebuild their nationhood after being reduced to living in squalid concentration camps during the Anglo-Boer War.

Fourie says that he wanted to help students understand the different perspectives of South African history – the traditional Afrikaner perspective on, or version of, history, and English-liberal, Marxist, labour-union and black perspectives. Each of these shape much of South Africa's politics and events, and each have their own validity and appeal.

'Understanding that history is a complex phenomenon and that there is not only one history is a liberating thing,' Fourie says.

In 1960, Vereeniging once again caught the world's attention when 69 people were killed in Sharpeville, a settlement near the town, on 21 March. Police opened fire on peaceful demonstrators who had been protesting against the extension of the apartheid pass law to women.

Writer André Brink, an anti-apartheid Afrikaner who was studying in Paris in 1960, remembers hearing news of the Sharpeville massacre while he was in the Luxembourg Gardens. 'In the modern experience of South Africa, in the unfolding of apartheid, this was the most massive, most cold-blooded, the most pernicious event we had yet to face,' Brink writes in his memoir, *A Fork in the Road*.[48]

Brink, grandson of an Anglo-Boer War veteran and son of a member of the Broederbond, recalls that he and other South African students in Paris received letters describing panic back home – 'all the firearms in town are sold out' – but also reassuring them that things would soon 'be back to normal'.[49]

De Wet's mother was born after Sharpeville, but she remembers another similar moment of panic among Afrikaners. On the eve of South Africa's first all-race elections, on 27 April 1994, things were never to return to what isolated Afrikaner communities would think of as 'normal'. Oosthuizen recalls that before the historic vote, her husband had stocked up with lots of tinned-food supplies. Among certain white South Africans at the time, fear was widespread that society as they knew it would collapse – stores would be looted; black domestic workers would demand to take over the homes where they worked. But many white South Africans today are reluctant to talk about their feeling of panic then.

'I remember that,' Oosthuizen says of the sense of panic. 'But not clearly.'

Oosthuizen says she voted in 1994 but does not remember for whom, it was so long ago.

De Wet, who is very close to his mother, says he has learnt something of the possibility of transformation by listening to stories of her childhood. 'If you have something like that, my mom's history, there's no other way to see it,' he says.

His mother describes her early days as 'very unsettled'. Although she was a high-school dropout, she has sent one son to university, and soon expects to send a second. According to De Wet, 'coming from where she came from, and getting me to where I am now' is proof that change can be made by an effort of will, in individual lives and, more broadly, in society. 'All of the things that happened . . . she could have sat down and cried. But she didn't,' De Wet says.

Lizelle Oosthuizen grew up in the Vaal Triangle. At 38, she has never been on a plane. Her mother, who according to family stories was depressed, committed suicide when Oosthuizen was 11. She was the only child still at home. Her father drank too much and struggled to care for his daughter after his wife died. Oosthuizen lived with him for a while, and was then sent to her older sister, one of her three brothers, then back to her father. 'I had no place to go; I had no house that I could call my parents' house.'

She went to six different high schools. At 16 she left school, got a job at a café and shared an apartment with a friend. It was a bid for independence and stability. The next year, she was pregnant.

'I'm kind of a mistake, sitting in front of you,' De Wet says. 'But, I think, a good one.'

Oosthuizen refused to marry her son's father. She thought he was immature and too attached to his mother. But she did name her son after him, so Eddie carries his father's surname.

Despite her circumstances, Oosthuizen says she never worried about how she would raise her son on her own. 'I think when you're young, you assume you can do anything,' she says. 'When I think of it today, I don't even know how I got through. I never had anyone to show me. I decided I was going to be the best mom I could be.'

She saved for what she would need to bring up her baby, and refused to ask for anything from the father. She worked until a week before her son was born on 23 April 1992. That makes De Wet just two years short of being a 'born-free' – born after apartheid.

After her son was born, Oosthuizen moved in with a sister and found work at a dental practice where she is still a receptionist. She married the father of De Wet's younger brother, Willie. Her husband drank too much, and was prone to violence when drunk. He once shot at her. He committed suicide when De Wet was eight.

Oosthuizen was strict when the boys were young. She was also determined that her sons would not be shunted from one school to another, as she had been. Her first apartment was a short walk from Vereeniging's main junior school, which was next door to the main high school. When Oosthuizen was able to move to a better part of town, she drove her sons to school rather than send them to a different one.

Sitting in her home with me, she flips through photo albums of her sons that record their growing up. Oosthuizen once worked as a taxi driver to earn extra money to make sure her sons had what they needed and what they wanted. She wanted them to have the education that she had missed out on. Now, saddled with expenses that include De Wet's university fees, she works at weekends as a DJ.

'How cool is she?' says her proud son.

Proud son, proud mom. She expects De Wet to be the first in the family to graduate from university. 'He was a very clever little boy,' she says, looking at a photo of a very young De Wet in cap and gown for his pre-primary leaving ceremony in 1998. 'A go-getter – always wanted to do everything. And he always wanted to be first.'

When I think of family trauma in South Africa, I am also reminded of one of the darkest legacies of the nation's divided past. The apartheid government decreed where blacks could work and where they could live. Typically, black men would spend most of their lives working in mines and factories in the cities, far from their families in the rural areas. Away from their families, they lived in hostels that were little more than warehouses for sleeping. The legacy of this is far-reaching: generations of black boys grew into men with no model for how to participate in raising a family because their fathers were absent.

A broken home is hardly just a black thing, however. De Wet, who says it can be difficult 'to talk to someone who comes from a perfect family', has formed a particular bond with an F1 colleague who is coloured. She grew up without a father at home and is as devoted to her mother as De Wet is to his.

Of the dozen Kovsies who took part in the UFS programme in Texas at the same time as De Wet, I am aware of four who are children of divorced or separated parents, and one whose father died when he was young. They are from all races. The sample may be too small to draw statistically accurate conclusions. However, a UFS member of staff who has spent time with De Wet and the other F1 programme students has noticed something about those who have emerged from broken homes. 'You often find that students that come from broken communities respond better to the programme,' the university administrator tells me. Those who are from more stable backgrounds are 'not used to having to overcome' life's challenges.

De Wet makes the same point, albeit less academically: 'In a sense, it's weird that in life you get the people that have gone through a difficult time that stand out. They don't want to sit in a corner and have people feeling sorry for them.'

De Wet would probably list expressing regrets about his fatherless childhood under the heading 'feeling sorry for yourself'. Despite this, Oosthuizen knows it's not quite true, as her son claims, that she was the only parent he needed. His father moved away from Vereeniging soon after De Wet was born, but returned when he was about 10. Once, in a grocery store, his mother pointed out the man – and his family – to her young son. Later, without telling his mother, De Wet wrote to his father asking to meet. For several years, Eddie spent every other weekend with his father, two half-brothers and stepmother. But he always felt like an outsider, and the relationship with his father fizzled out.

'One day he told me he wasn't going there any more,' Oosthuizen says. 'I think he came to realise that his father's not really interested.'

His father lives just a few kilometres away in Vereeniging, but Eddie hasn't spoken to him in years, although his father does regularly transfer money into a bank account for his son, and Oosthuizen makes sure De Wet thanks him by SMS.

'Anybody would miss a parent,' Oosthuizen says. She remembers her son reaching out to favourite teachers and the fathers of his friends as surrogate fathers.

When it was time to apply for university, her son showed an interest in UFS. Oosthuizen, an autodidact and avid reader, sought books and articles about the university. She found out about its halls of residence and when she took her son on a pre-enrolment visit she advised him against his first choice. It was a res too steeped in tradition, she believes, and she was concerned he would be uncomfortable in a place that had been home to generations of wealthy, influential Afrikaners. De Wet instead chose Armentum, the residence that, with a name change, had tried to turn over a new leaf on its past.

Oosthuizen had read about racism at the university, but says she was never worried that her son would fall in with young Afrikaners who were clinging to the traditions of apartheid. 'I think Eddie makes good choices,' she says. 'He's not influenced easily.'

She's glad that De Wet came into contact with Jonathan Jansen and enrolled on his F1 leadership programme. Oosthuizen has seen a change in her son since he returned from the US. He's more mature, more certain of where he wants to go, more aware of the sacrifices made to get him where he is. 'Sometimes, South African kids can be a bit selfish. Life out there is very tough and they don't always realise that. I think Eddie's seen the bigger picture,' she says.

'There are big things out there,' she says, referring to the opportunities she believes her son has – and which she did not – to travel, to learn and to lead.

When her son was in high school, Oosthuizen was sometimes perplexed by how his teachers and principals took advantage of his willingness to do things and display leadership. She used to intervene and request that some of his responsibilities be lifted. She doesn't worry, however, about the tasks he has been asked to take on at university since returning from the US, a trip she views as a bonus.

'If you receive something,' she says, 'you should always give back.'

If De Wet found a mentor in Jansen, Oosthuizen has as well.

When her boys were growing up, their headmasters could make her feel small. She thought the vice chancellor of the university would also be arrogant and unapproachable. She still remembers the first time she saw Jansen: he was in the audience at a student performance, and obviously enjoying the singing and dancing on stage. 'I was so surprised to see him there, right in the middle of the kids,' she says.

De Wet talks about Jansen a lot, his mother says. She knows the rector sets aside time to speak with and listen to the students. 'I feel Eddie's safe there,' she says. 'If you need to talk to somebody, it's always nice to know there's a door open to you.'

She reads Jansen's columns and essays published in newspapers and magazines, and follows news about him on television. 'I love Prof. Jansen. I just love his face. It looks like a grandfather's face to me,' she says. 'He can be a father figure to any child. He's coloured, but he can be a father figure to any child. The kids today, they don't see colour.'

Oosthuizen is comfortable with the apartheid-era race classifications of her time. She refers to the black woman who cleans her house four days a week as a 'girl'. When asked about race relations in her own life, she relates that the 'girls' who clean her office and prepare tea for her and her co-workers call her '*skattie*', an Afrikaans term of endearment. The black man who makes his living washing cars in the parking lot at her office calls her '*tannie*' (auntie).

Although Oosthuizen never went to school with black South Africans, there are one or two dark-skinned faces in the photos of De Wet's class at his crèche, a few more in junior school and still more in high school.

'South Africa's changed,' she says. 'I've got black neighbours now.'

The children of her neighbours, black and white alike, play rugby together and go to school together. When she drove to university to help her son settle in at the start of his first year, she recounts how his res mates, black and white, helped her unload the supplies from the car. All called her *tannie*.

A few months later, De Wet brought one of his new university friends home for the weekend. She explains how he had never mentioned to his mother that his friend was a coloured young man. She assumes her son just felt race was not important enough to raise, and while she says she found that surprising, she is quick to add that she did not feel she was being pushed out of her comfort zone when she was presented with a coloured visitor. She was struck, she said, to see the two of them in her son's room the first day, the dark skin of the visitor sharply contrasting with her son's pale skin, but the two of them were as at ease with each other as brothers.

She describes apartheid as 'a time of racism'. Her son escaped that burden, and she sees the timing of his birth as another opportunity he has that she missed. She can imagine him one day working for a black boss, she says. 'Eddie's always got along with all kinds of people. Some of his best friends are black people.'

De Wet, however, looks back now on what he sees as years of missed opportunity at Hoërskool Vereeniging. It was an integrated high school, but whites stuck with whites, blacks with blacks, coloureds with coloureds, Indians with Indians, he says.

After his taste of Texas, De Wet is considering studying medicine in the US. But he also wants to bring back what he learnt in Texas to South Africa, including the confidence he found among students in College Station. He dreams of one day having a practice in Bloemfontein.

In an email littered with exclamation marks that De Wet sent upon returning to Bloemfontein to a Texas university administrator who had been a mentor there, he says that he learnt

> what it means to be an adaptable person, as society changes daily, and if we want to survive we need to keep up, and be willing to take on challenges as true leaders! The respect, pride and openness the Aggies have towards one another, the diversity, and the interest to learn and engage in different situations to grow personally was something that stood out for me!

Although de Wet has been infected by a sense of the possibility of reinvention, on the UFS campus the different races still stick within their own groups to a large extent. But Jansen has challenged the students to confront their and their parents' assumptions about race. Posters around the campus showing bright young faces invite students to apply for the F1 programme. The posters seem to promise a new sense of self, and of how to relate to others.

8. The weight of history

'm on a musical meander, visiting the UFS halls of residence as their members rehearse for an event known as Serenade, at which choirs compete with elaborate performances reminiscent of Broadway or a scene from the US TV series *Glee*. De Wet has told me how aggressively and creatively the choirs formed of members of each residence compete to be named as the top Serenade performers. As I go from rehearsal to rehearsal, I can't help thinking that I'm watching stylised gestures and dance steps that have been handed down from generation to generation within a res – though it's also clear the American pop culture is having an influence on the song choices and arrangements.

Black and white students are practising together, though hardly in proportions I would call representative. I'm glimpsing and hearing what draws many students to res life: camaraderie and a sense of history. The residences are still very much the heart of campus life at UFS. So transforming them is at the heart of any effort to make the university a more inclusive place.

When he first took over as rector, Jansen found that black students at one residence were forced to take part in a decades-old tradition of honouring the bust of an Afrikaner founding father. 'There, you have black students bowing to a white guy they have no connection to. It's racist,' he says. 'What has meaning for you doesn't have meaning for the other guy. I'm trying to change the things that are borderline criminal and barbaric.'

I am also reminded of an American historian I met during a conference in Bloemfontein and of her exasperation at some of the difficulties faced by South Africans. She was disheartened by what she calls the 'conversational racism' she heard among students on campus. She also noticed black students wearing ties emblazoned with the logo of the residence named after J. B. M. Hertzog, the Anglo-Boer War general and South Africa's prime minister from 1924 to 1939, a period that saw legislation passed that severely restricted the rights of black South Africans.

The historian questioned students about what they thought of the symbols they wore and the monuments they walked past on their way to class. 'They kind of laugh it off,' she told me.

While the women's residences have long histories and their own rituals, they are not as rigidly tradition-bound as the men's. When black students first began arriving in large numbers, university staff say they found the women's residences more flexible about welcoming black women, and racial integration was less fraught in the women's residences.

Armentum used to be named after Hendrik Verwoerd, the former South African prime minister known as the chief architect of apartheid. In 2006 the university, in its symbolic as well as practical search for ways to ease racial tensions, renamed the residence. The men of Armentum gather every Monday evening for their house meeting. De Wet introduced me as a guest, and they were happy to allow me to attend one of these meetings.

At the meeting, I saw the more senior students enter first. They gather around in a large room dominated by a billboard-sized oil painting of a herd of elephants. The first-year residents enter the Armentum meetings after their seniors. The first years all have neat, closely cropped haircuts, according to house rules. All are dressed in regulation khaki pants, blue blazers and ties bearing the elephant emblem of the house. However, some of the older students are in pyjamas, as if to underline the sartorial freedom they have earned after completing their first year. But even among them, there's a sense of conformity.

The meetings open with a prayer and end with the house anthem, in which the men of Armentum laud, in their fine voices, their sense of purpose and unity. The tune brings to mind a lively march. Or a drinking song.

Between the prayer and the song, there are announcements about recruiting visits by banks and insurance companies, a call to donate to a university programme to help feed poor students, and lots of joking about drinking and women. Black residents are by far in the minority, a reminder that the university's hallowed residences remain largely segregated. The black men at the house meeting sit together in groups here and there, but they don't hold back when it comes to participating in the proceedings, and several take seats at the front table reserved for members of the committee who run the residence's business.

But Armentum has an elephant in the room, literally as well figuratively. It is out of sight, behind locked doors. There is a room that houses the residence museum. The polite Armentum residents find the keys to the two doors, one an accordion of steel bars, another of wood, to open up the museum and usher me in after I have asked to have a look around. Inside there are mementoes from the era when the residence was still named after the former prime minister. Among them is a huge photograph of Verwoerd that once hung where the painting of the elephants now has pride of place in the common room. The photograph is too large for any of the walls of the small room set aside for the museum, so it is mounted on the ceiling. Verwoerd stares down, a half smile on his face. I think how I might feel if I were to wander into a back room in a campus dormitory in Texas and found myself confronted with a giant Confederate flag, its stars and bars perhaps a symbol of defiance to some, but, to me, a reminder of slavery and an icon of racism.

In 1961, while Verwoerd was prime minister, a white-ruled South African republic independent of Britain was born. A year earlier, British Prime Minister Harold Macmillan had addressed the South African Parliament, telling lawmakers he believed a 'wind of change' was sweeping away colonial rule across the continent, clearing the way for independent African states led by Africans. Verwoerd responded with a passionate articulation of Afrikaner nationalism:

> We call ourselves Europeans, but actually we represent the white men of Africa. They are the people ... who brought civilisation here, who made the present developments of black nationalists possible. And the white man came to Africa, perhaps to trade,

in some cases, perhaps, to bring the gospel; [he] has remained to stay. [White Africans,] particularly in this southernmost portion of Africa, have such a stake here that this is our only motherland, we have nowhere else to go.[50]

In the museum, display cabinets hold old yearbooks in which the faces are white. The cabinets are full of awards and photographs, tributes to former residents who achieved fame in sports or other areas. A wooden plaque bears the words of the old house song, which referred to the men of Verwoerd, not the men of Armentum. On a wall there is a black-and-white photograph, faded to shades of grey, of Betsie Verwoerd with her husband. Hendrik Verwoerd was stabbed to death in 1966 in Cape Town by a parliamentary messenger who was later deemed to have been insane.

As apartheid ended, Betsie Verwoerd was among a minority of Afrikaners who refused to accept the proposition that the races should live together. The prime minister's widow and a few hundred others moved to the white Afrikaner settlement of Orania, whose name harks back to the Orange Free State. They went on their own, without the low-paid black maids, gardeners and farm workers on whom the apartheid economy had been built.

In a gesture of reconciliation, Nelson Mandela, then president, visited Betsie Verwoerd in Orania in 1995. Newspaper photographs show Mandela lending the widow a steadying hand as she read a speech declaring her belief that Afrikaners needed an independent homeland of their own. Earlier, she had shared coffee and cake in private with Mandela.

Although it is common to hear white South Africans express the fearful uncertainty that led Betsie Verwoerd to flee to Orania, only a few hundred ever joined her in that small Karoo community.

What is the purpose of the museum? The Armentum students tell me that the first impulse when the house name was changed was to preserve the past, that there was an unwillingness to simply dump tradition in the bin. A friendly guide also explains that looking into the room gives one a chance to see how far Armentum and the university have moved on. The guide has been at Armentum for four years, long enough to be a link to some of the residents who set up the museum. As he leads a tour of the room, he uses the word 'shameful' several times as he speaks of apartheid.

Surely, I think, few conversations can be started among young South Africans by mementoes and stories that are kept locked away, dusted off occasionally for a visitor to look at. The reluctance to have hard conversations about the past could be read as reluctance to talk frankly about the present.

When I ask De Wet about the museum, he says people don't really visit it. 'It scratches open a lot of wounds,' he says. 'It's very small, and it's not really relevant any more.'

For better or for worse, the Afrikaner nationalism espoused by leaders like Verwoerd shaped South Africa. De Wet says his generation wants to break down the barriers erected in the past, and he believes that means abandoning some history. De Wet recognises that UFS is trying to make 'a definite transformation towards integration', and that the institution is encouraging its students to think differently about living in a diverse society.

'If I hadn't come to UFS, I wouldn't have had this opportunity to broaden my horizon and think about it differently. I know that colour is not supposed to be an identity,' he says. 'You have to be unified in something else, something bigger that you have in common.'

During his visit to the US, De Wet wrote in an email to a reporter that he was experiencing 'a different perception on diversity here in the USA, not only race as we usually classify it. I am starting to process information, and getting better at listening to others and taking in rather than just jumping to conclusions without thinking them through.'

De Wet is an optimist and equates pessimism with the past:

> People who are negative, they're stuck in the past. They don't see that there's a possibility for change. They've already made up their mind. They don't want to imagine better. They just let the negative take over everything. There's noise in their ears. And we have this silence, because we don't let it bother us.

He and the other South Africans with whom he travelled to Texas are learning to see the world differently, he says. 'We can make a huge difference. We're looking at the future. If you want to move forward, you should stop thinking about the past.'

Easy to say, but history towers over South Africa's landscape and is embedded in the names of its people and places. It's not a room that you can leave, switch off the light and shut the door.

Willy Nel, a psychologist who trains future teachers in the university's education department, took on extra university duties in mid-2012, during De Wet's second year at UFS. Nel became master of Armentum, a staff position not usually held by professors, but a role that Jansen's administration would like to see developed more in order to provide a bridge between students and academics. Nel says he applied for the job out of a desire 'to become involved in the messy affairs of the university'.

Nel, who had been teaching at North-West University, was attracted to UFS because under Jansen the university had developed a reputation for fostering research. He saw the job at Armentum in part as a research opportunity, saying he wanted to document what he saw and experienced among his charges, with the aim of writing about it himself or making his notes available to other academics who share his interests.

'I'm investigating the change process,' Nel explains. 'Because the world has changed. South Africa has changed.'

The residences at UFS, however, have been slow to change, despite repeated attempts by the administration to make them more representative and to ensure new ideals are embraced as part of their culture. Some might dismiss the residences as irrelevant, as only about 12 per cent of the student population live on campus today, but their historic role as the centre of campus life, dating from the time when most university students lived on campus, means they cannot be ignored, Nel explains. The first thing a visitor sees upon driving through the main campus gate is a group of low, brick-built residences, ranged like pawns before the main administration block and classroom buildings.

In the 2012 academic year, Nel moved into an apartment attached to Armentum. At his first house meeting, he reminded the residents of the university's commitment to diversity and tolerance.

Nel wears his hair in a mop of dreadlocks, most of them short, with one long lock stretching down his back. This makes him a contrasting figure among the young men of his house with their short haircuts.

In the 1980s, Nel had been among the first black students admitted to Stellenbosch University. While he identifies himself as black, his light-coloured skin and ease with Afrikaans might lead other South Africans to label him as coloured. Nel's first job, before he went on to study for his doctorate and teach at university level, was teaching Afrikaans as a first-language to high-school students in the coloured communities of the Northern Cape. He addressed his first house meeting at Armentum in English.

Nel tells me that he sees the use of Afrikaans in the reses as an attempt to impose old ways on new students, most of whom are black and unlikely to speak the language. He also describes the rules about how first-year students should dress and wear their hair as throwbacks to an authoritarian era which now have no place on a post-apartheid campus:

> First years should be colleagues. First years shouldn't be a lesser species of men. They should have freedom of choice. For instance, about the clothes they wear. What if those young men don't want to wear jackets and ties? They have no choice in the matter. That's a form of abuse. And its psycho-politically not on. I will challenge things, and I will go into real debates with the students. I'm not going in there naively thinking it's a smooth ride.

When De Wet arrived at Armentum, he was annoyed at the way he and other first years were treated. 'I'm not a slave,' he says. He has little respect for people who scream at him, telling him that he has to fetch them a beer.

But he didn't fight it. Instead, he threw himself into the activities at his residence, particularly the singing and performance groups that compete against other reses. De Wet has been an avid performer since his junior-school days. He also joined the Armentum social committee, one of the few res groups where the voices of first-year students are welcome.

De Wet is not the only one to realise it may be impossible to change the residence culture – or at least to change it quickly. Nel found that his first challenge as new housemaster was getting his residents to talk frankly. The week he moved into Armentum, a visiting American student of Hispanic descent moved out after a dispute with a South African room-mate. Nel said that in his attempt to determine what had been the problem, Armentum men struck him as resisting the possibility that race or racism could have played a role in the altercation.

'Racial incidents will have to be tackled from a racial point of view,' Nel says. 'The word "race" figures in my vocabulary. I'm not colour-blind.'

Nel was aware of the house's history. By coincidence, he was born in 1968, the year the residence that would become Armentum was built and named after Verwoerd. And there's another coincidence: Verwoerd was a psychologist, as is Nel.

'That's an ironic twist of history,' Nel says.

History indeed has a habit of throwing up ironies, but also parallels from which lessons can be drawn.

9. Dancing in Bloemfontein

Jessica Guerra, one of the students who had hosted a UFS student visiting Texas on the F1 programme, came to South Africa. She hit the clubs in Bloemfontein and she was amazed at what she was seeing. To be more precise, she was amazed at what she was not seeing.

'No one would touch one another. At all. They wouldn't even get that close to each other.'

There were none of the public displays of affection that would go unnoticed on a dance floor back home in the US, where, as Guerra puts it, 'people dance with far fewer boundaries'.

The young South Africans who showed her around town were the UFS students to whom she became close a year earlier when they visited Texas A&M, where Guerra is studying international relations with a minor in business.

I decided to seek Guerra out in Texas because the effort she had made to visit South Africa impressed many of the South African students I interviewed, and certainly impressed me. I also admire the way she mixes the traditional and the progressive, the personal and the political, in an entirely individual way.

At the Bloemfontein club, Guerra tells me, she had turned to her hosts and asked why people weren't dancing together. They told her that you just don't do that here. You just don't.

In Texas, the South Africans had survived their taste of American night life at a gay-friendly club, Halo, though it may not have been clear to them that the club is something of an anomaly in a state known for its conservatism. Back on campus at Texas A&M University, I heard gay, lesbian and other students who don't fit the state's norm speak of verbal harassment or worse at the hands of fellow students.

TAMU is the kind of traditional place where young men go down on one knee to propose to their girlfriends under the Century Tree, a campus landmark, while teary-eyed onlookers pause on their way to the library to applaud. Guerra explains that, according to university lore, you will marry the person with whom you walk in the tree's shade, but you will never marry, the myth goes, if you carelessly pass alone under its branches.

The Century Tree stands near the campus square, the site of the monthly Silver Taps ceremony. Guerra is deeply impressed by this ceremony, which is a tribute to students who have died. She describes the solemn mood that accompanies the ceremonial steps made by the Corps of Cadets, an institution established in the early days of the university. The corps is organised along military lines and prepares students for possible careers in the armed forces.

At the Memorial Student Center (MSC), a sprawling, stone-and-glass building, co-eds reading Chaucer and cadets in camouflage can find common ground over a cup of coffee. Signs at the entrance remind visitors that it is dedicated to 'all Aggies who have given their lives in defence of their country in any war, past or future'.

The signs go on to observe: 'The students of Texas A&M have formally adopted two traditions designed to honor the fallen: removing caps when entering the building, and staying off the grass around MSC.' And the students do remove their caps as they enter the building through its main doors, each aligned under a one-word motto set in steel lettering: 'loyalty', 'respect', 'honor', 'integrity', 'leadership'.

Guerra, who is family-oriented and idealistic, loves her fellow TAMU students for the way they embrace tradition and old-fashioned values, even though the glorification of things military can trouble her. It is these traits that have helped cement the university's conservative reputation.

In many ways, Guerra represents a new kind of student at TAMU. She is from a city, not a small farming town. Her father is Hispanic, and although Hispanic Americans were never formally barred from TAMU as black Americans were, they have historically not been particularly welcomed. And woman were not formally admitted until the 1960s.

That night she spent clubbing in Bloemfontein, Guerra saw that a label like 'conservative' is a matter of degree and context. It was just one of many labels she would find herself confronting and contemplating during her stay in South Africa.

Her trip to Bloemfontein was not Guerra's first visit to Africa. During high school, she went to Uganda to attend the digging of a village well for which she had raised funds. The project shows that, even as a teenager, she had a maturity beyond her age and youthful looks. She also has an international outlook, compassion and determination. Her ambitions include saving the world – as well as having a large family.

To help alleviate the plight of the villagers in Uganda who lacked easy access to water, she and four school friends gathered to brainstorm fundraising ideas. They came up with designs for T-shirts featuring outlines of the African continent, had them printed and sold enough to raise $12 000, which they donated to an international development group to finance the well.

Later, when a TAMU professor mentioned a study-abroad programme in Namibia, Guerra was keen, given her tie to Africa. The idea took firmer root when the South Africans arrived. 'I spent so much time with them, and I got to know them so well,' she says. 'These students were just wonderful. I know that's just an adjective, but these students have a life to them.'

She promised she would return the visit, so she looked into TAMU's programme in Namibia. She would be able to earn credits toward her degree, taking classes from TAMU professors who would travel with the group. She would be able to contribute to environmental projects in Namibia, and then she could tag on a visit to her UFS friends in Bloemfontein, just a few hours' flight from Windhoek.

The trip would cost nearly $10 000. She was granted a $1 500 study-abroad scholarship from the university, then she set to work finding other sponsors to fund the balance: 'I am 20 years old, and I have decided to change the world,' Guerra wrote in a letter she sent to potential sponsors. 'These two sentences alone may give the impression that I am a wide-eyed college kid with a romantic view of the world; this assumption is far from the truth,' Guerra continues. 'While I know one person cannot change the world, each of us doing our part can accomplish the positive change we need.' In her letter, she described what she had already done for the Ugandan villagers, and the courses she would be pursuing in Namibia. She included photographs from her visit to Uganda, to show that it wasn't just some day dream that she had: 'I have a history of following through.'

With each request for sponsorship, she included a stamped, addressed envelope for donors to send cheques. Guerra says that she wanted to link her sponsorship proposal to the fact that this was an investment in the future, and not just the future of Africa:

> I made it relatable to the future of Texas. I told them we were going to be working on projects and issues that Texans are going to face in the future. Especially water issues, conservation – we're going to be facing these more and more as Texans. And the Namibians are facing those already. Just because I'm in another country, on another continent, doesn't mean I can't learn something very valuable and bring it back. It's not just for me. It's for the future.

In the end, half her trip was funded by donations.

Because she also included a trip to South Africa, her itinerary was different from those of the professors and students who took part in the study-abroad programme. They car-pooled from College Station to Houston, then headed to different flights, all bound for Namibia. 'I felt like such an explorer, and so independent. And sleep deprived,' Guerra says, laughing at herself.

She found her maturity and independence were tested from the start of the trip. A fledgling vegan, Guerra was used to chatting with like-minded friends back home about articles they'd read about the incidence of lactose intolerance among Americans, or whether cattle was being raised humanely by the meat industry. Many of the Texans with whom she travelled to Namibia, she discovered, had grown up on their families' dairy and cattle farms. They viewed her diet, as well as her attempts to explain and justify it, as a challenge.

'My classmates grew up on farms, and this is why their families were able to eat, and have a house,' she concedes. She tries to avoid confrontation. She respects her classmates as part of a tradition that has fed the world, efficiently and productively, for generations. But she also wants to get across her perspective on these issues.

A city girl who'd never even gardened before arriving in College Station, Guerra discovered a personal interest in agriculture at TAMU. She volunteers once a week at a student-run organic farm just beyond the buildings where TAMU students study cutting-edge agriculture. The farm supplies TAMU's dining halls and food banks for the poor.

She pauses as we walk across the TAMU campus to show her admiration for a drip irrigation system in a flower bed outside a classroom building. Later, she gestures with pride at a photo of Nobel laureate Norman Borlaug, the late American plant scientist who helped impoverished nations develop disease-resistant, highly productive food crops, earning him the title of Father of the Green Revolution. Guerra follows the impassioned debates on campus on issues such as whether genetically modified crops are safe. She believes the future of the planet depends on sustainable agriculture, and that everyone interested in farming should share ideas.

'I'm not the kind of person who's just going to go out and say, "Drinking milk is bad for you" and start bad-mouthing,' she says. 'I want to learn more and I want to share what I think. If I'd had my friends with me in Namibia to back me up on facts, to jump in when I didn't have the words, then it would have been different. It would have been what I'm used to.'

Guerra was challenged to reconsider her perspective and her approach when she went on the study-abroad programme. And she came to see the benefits of that:

> Just being immersed in such a different group helped me grow a lot. It made me realise that I need to understand a lot more, not just about science. I need to learn it from other viewpoints. I need to understand how to communicate with people who are going to think that I'm against them. Even if I am against them, I need to understand how to work with them.

That lesson was still fresh at the end of the five-week session in Namibia. The TAMU professors and other students headed back to the US. Guerra headed to South Africa.

To prepare for her trip to South Africa, Guerra had read up on South African history. It struck her how recent the apartheid era was, even if it had not been directly experienced by the South Africans she knew. By contrast, in her own nation's history, slavery and racial segregation were much more distant in time.

'Think about what the US went through, and how many years it took to get to a place where racism is much less,' says Guerra. And yet, she points out, 'we still face so many racial issues. You still see the effects of it.'

Guerra says that she couldn't imagine that South African society would be normal so soon after the end of apartheid. 'This is the first generation that they can really start working toward equality and a brighter future.'

Guerra's own experience, she believes, helps her understand what it might mean to be a South African because she also found that many of her assumptions about her place in the world had been suddenly challenged. 'I come from San Antonio, a city that has a majority Hispanic population,' she says. 'I knew, maybe, five Asian and five black people and some white people when I grew up. That was the whole cultural spread. Which, of course, I was comfortable with, because I'm half Hispanic. I was just used to seeing Mexican people.'

Then, she enrolled at TAMU, a campus where two-thirds of the 50 000 students are white. 'I realised, for the first time, I was in a minority,' Guerra says.

Even her white friends from San Antonio were taken aback when they arrived together as first-year students. 'I remember they asked, "Where are all the Mexicans?"'

As a young undergraduate, one of her first outings was to a dance at a bar with a group of friends. She saw her white friends from San Antonio transformed, in jeans and cowboy hats. 'They put on the clothes and walked out onto the dance floor and looked like they'd been here their whole lives,' Guerra says. 'But when I went onto the floor, I felt really out of place. I'm short and Hispanic. I felt really uncomfortable.'

After the dance, she called home. 'I know I'll fit in eventually,' she told her mother. 'But I just feel so out of place and out-numbered. Here, everyone is so different-looking. They fit in, and I don't.'

Her mom advised her to give it more time, and to find groups and activities where she could fit in. Guerra says she decided to trust her mother. And she made another decision: 'I remember making a conscious decision that I wasn't going to think of my-self as a minority. I wasn't going to see myself in that light. I wasn't going to let myself be a victim of anything,' she says.

During her two weeks in Bloemfontein, Guerra lived in a house off campus that Lara Brown shared with friends. Brown, an occupational-therapy student at UFS, had stayed with Guerra in the Texan's apartment when the Kovsies had been in College Station.

TAMU students are proud of their reputation for friendliness, entering rooms with loud greetings, which they expect to be reciprocated with equal enthusiasm. South Africans also consider a warm welcome a basic courtesy, and Guerra's friends made sure she got a taste of local hospitality. Guerra made time to visit the student bars and attend braais.

She went to the offices of *Irawa*, the UFS official student newspaper, and attended classes. As a former medical student, she was especially intrigued when she saw South African medical students studying cadavers. On these visits, she realised that the facilities and technology available to students at UFS lagged far behind what she was used to at TAMU.

TAMU has sometimes struggled financially, and as a state university has needed the support of politicians. The endowments received by TAMU and other Texan universities, however, have been boosted by oil revenue – some oil wells are on university land.

Guerra's campus today is in the midst of a construction boom, with new student dormitories being built, the expansion of a unit where high-tech research is conducted, and the construction of a pedestrian tunnel to facilitate travel between new and old parts of the sprawling institution. An expanded student centre, equipped with a 16 000-square-foot ballroom and high-speed data lines and wireless internet access, was opened in 2012. A recreation centre, where Guerra took up archery when she returned from South Africa, has indoor rock-climbing facilities, a 50-metre pool and a diving well.

In South Africa, UFS is also intent on improving its infrastructure, in part because new buildings can help root new traditions. There are plans to transform residences like Reitz, now infamous for the racist video, and professors are being encouraged to play a more active mentoring role in the residences. New residences will not have the baggage of tradition that the old ones carry. Some may even be co-ed, a radical innovation at conservative UFS.

When Guerra had planned her trip, she had contacted UFS officials, among them the dean of students. She wanted to find ways of making herself productive while she was there. The dean of students and others spoke of efforts to ensure the small number of students who had gained so much from brief visits abroad were able to sustain their energy and commitment. It was crucial that they could share their experience for the greater good of their university.

Guerra was therefore recruited as a kind of one-woman survey team. She was a peer to whom the students could relate, but also an outsider who might see something from a different angle. She focused on Kovsies from the F1 programme she hadn't met before, those who had travelled to universities in Europe and Japan, and to US campuses other than TAMU. She talked with the South African students in groups, and began to piece together a picture of their concerns.

The South Africans of all races Guerra had met in College

Station had seemed so at ease with each that it was only when she got to Bloemfontein that she began to realise that apartheid is still a fresh scar. 'This is one of the first generations not to be around during apartheid,' she says. 'They really are the future.'

She saw an impatience that may have struck a personal chord, an impatience often expressed as self-criticism. 'The reason that they're hard on themselves is because they are the people who can change things. They are the leaders. Leaders are always hard on themselves. People who have a vision for something better are always critical. They know things can be better.'

Among other things, she heard from some of the students who had been abroad as part of the first F1 group that they felt replaced by those who went with the next intake, instead of forming part of one unified community.

I hear something similar from economics student Nyakallo 'SJ' Scheepers, who speaks of how difficult it was for the first students who were part of F1. They had no foundation to build on, he says. His group was the second to go.

'We're still in the early stages,' he says. 'What we should do is collaborate with the previous F1s and make that strong foundation. We should understand that things don't change quickly. You have to take time and have patience.'

Setting a realistic agenda for F1 would also help students who already have busy agendas, he believes. 'Before I went to F1, I had goals, academic goals,' Scheepers says, adding that those goals will remain his priority despite his commitment to F1.

Scheepers is the first person in his family to go to university.

He is proud of his relatives, including his older sister and older brother, who never had a chance to continue their education. 'They just worked hard and found a way out,' he says.

Scheepers's ambitions grew while he was in Texas. Warren Chalklen, the former Wits student who went to study at TAMU, was so impressed with Scheepers that he encouraged him to consider graduate studies in the US.

But Scheepers also wants to help push for change at UFS, as F1 students are expected to. He finds inspiration in theology student Mias Nortier. It's not surprising that Nortier, who is white, and Scheepers, who is black, grew close while in Texas together. Both are soft-spoken and reserved, and both are older students. Nortier took up Sotho studies after returning from his trip to Texas, deciding he needed a black African language as a bridge to fellow South Africans. Scheepers says that is the kind of small step that can have lasting impact.

'Mias is doing something to understand other cultures, to understand the Sotho language and people. Even if he only does that, it's a contribution,' says Scheepers, who grew up speaking Sotho at home and English at school, and can get by in Afrikaans.

Scheepers is trying to take a personal step of his own, pushing himself to overcome his natural shyness and speak up more in F1 meetings, so that the time he can dedicate to the project is more likely to have an impact.

'I should be able to engage in dialogue. I really have to work on that skill,' Scheepers says. 'Those small things are the ones that matter at the end of the day.'

Scheepers reflects some of the concerns Guerra picked up on when she was in Bloemfontein, engaging with the students. Guerra comes from a school rich in tradition, ritual and structure, so she had some ideas about how to encourage unity and a sense of purpose at UFS. She identified the need for a formal F1 alumni group, led by a chairperson and other elected student leaders. 'It would be a support system. Not just a support system, but also a way to keep tracking the development of leadership in general at their university.'

Guerra belongs to several student-led groups at TAMU, and knows it takes a lot of work and dedication to get one off the ground. Though Guerra had ideas to share, she was wary of being seen as a know-it-all American. And she had been freshly sensitised by her experience in Namibia, where what she saw as her attempts to engage led to confrontation.

Her meetings with the F1 students culminated with a round table that drew together about 20 people. She opened the meeting by explaining herself: 'I'm doing this because I want to share my knowledge with you. I want to share as much as I possibly can, to help you in any way. If you don't use it at all, that's fine.'

Guerra was disturbed by some of what she saw during her stay in South Africa. While in College Station, the Kovsie visitors had seemed to her like a coherent unit: not coloureds or blacks or whites, but simply South Africans united by an inspiring vision. In Bloemfontein, however, Guerra saw students grouping themselves by race. Although the F1 students reached across the racial lines, they nevertheless perceived their differences in a way that was sometimes baffling to Guerra. Conversations were peppered with casual references to this friend's race, that friend's ethnic origins.

'They'd say words I didn't know, like "boer",' Guerra says, giving the label a credible Afrikaans accent. 'That means "farmer", right?' She knew the implications went beyond translation. She once pressed for an explanation, and was told that farmers 'wear weird socks'. Guerra could only laugh. 'I don't know what that means. I don't know what a farmer in South Africa looks like. There was a difference between black, coloured, white, Afrikaans, English. I could never tell who was what and they were surprised that I couldn't tell.'

The more Guerra listened, the more she became aware of the stereotypes that gave the labels a dark weight in her mind. 'The people who weren't Afrikaans, so, I guess, the English – they made comments about the Afrikaans accent.' They would say that it makes them sound dumb, she says.

'I know the people who would say that, and I know they don't mean it maliciously. But I still don't think that this is OK. I don't think it's working towards unity.'

Guerra has one set of grandparents from Mexico and another with roots in Europe. If a white friend were to mock the accent of one of her Mexican American relatives in the way she heard some South Africans comment on fellow South Africans, 'that would make me mad,' she says.

Mindful of the lesson she had learnt in Namibia about how

even the best-intentioned advice can be ill-judged when it comes from an outsider, Guerra didn't confront her South African friends about her reactions. Instead, she thought about what the South Africans might have heard in Texas.

And I thought of a story Brown told me about a day she had been in College Station, waiting for a campus bus. An American had gestured to a group of black students and mentioned they were probably athletes. An innocuous enough comment, probably even meant as a compliment at a college as sports-mad as TAMU. Indeed, some of the first black students to enrol at TAMU gained prominence as athletes, starting a tradition that continues today. But Brown, who is English-speaking and white, knew a stereotype when she heard one. She says minorities are in such small numbers at TAMU that white students there don't have to think about the reality of racism if they don't want to. 'Often, it's kind of swept under the carpet there,' she says. 'Here, we know it's present. We talk about it.'

When I meet Brown at the UFS campus, she is with accounting student Mano Rantsho. The two, who had travelled to Texas together, hold their heads close over a photo on a cellphone screen. The photograph shows Brown with her two little sisters adopted by her parents, one from a Xhosa background, the other Zulu.

'Cute!' Rantsho coos.

'My *oupa* is Afrikaans,' Brown says. 'So it was a struggle for him to initially come to terms with it. Now, he absolutely adores them,' she continues, explaining that her grandfather is the first to stand up for his new granddaughters when others question his interracial family.

Brown and others in her group brought their own complex perspectives to Texas, and back.

Guerra's visit to Bloemfontein was brief and she spent most of her time with F1 students. Alissa Leeds, however, spent more time there and met a broader range of UFS students. Leeds is a student from Appalachian State University, a North Carolina institution, which, like TAMU, hosted a group of students from UFS.

Leeds, like Guerra, was inspired by the South Africans she had met in the US. Her experience was that they were 'exceptional people and wonderful people'.

Too many other students, Leeds finds, however, are like a certain young Afrikaner she met one night in a bar. After three beers, she said, he felt comfortable enough to tell Leeds, who is white, what he really thought about race relations. He told her, 'If I could teach my kids and grandkids history, I would teach them to be racist and hate black people.'

Leeds says: 'That was my third day in Bloemfontein. I was so disgusted.'

Leeds, raised on a farm in North Carolina and one among many white southerners at her university, had to learn to navigate in a charged atmosphere at UFS. She found black students avoided her because they assumed she was Afrikaans, warming to her only when they learnt she was a foreigner. Afrikaans students were friendly until they realised she was not one of them, Leeds discovered.

'I felt like ET. It was really difficult in the beginning,' she tells me.

In the end, she found her place among certain UFS students who saw themselves as outsiders – a young white woman who stood out with hair dyed purple and in rocker clothes; a gay Afrikaner majoring in agriculture who told Leeds he had to steel himself for 30 minutes before facing class; a young woman with one Xhosa parent and one white, who was teased by black students for speaking Afrikaans.

'I feel for those students,' Leeds says. 'All I can say is, I get to leave, but they don't. We became friends with each other because we needed each other.'

She tried to immerse herself in campus life during what was initially intended to have been a year of study abroad. Leeds lived in one of the ritual-laden residences. She volunteered to usher at a rugby game. Residences and rugby are UFS traditions. However, she felt most engaged on the occasions she visited the International Institute for Studies in Race, Reconciliation and Social Justice, an organisation established in an attempt to forge new traditions at UFS.

The institute owes its existence to one of the most fraught events in UFS history: the production of the racist Reitz video. Jansen oversaw the inauguration of the institute. In the wake of the video, the mandate of the institute is to research how to heal a nation torn apart by apartheid.

Leeds joined other UFS students at several of the institute's lectures and talks. She attended them almost weekly for the first few months she was there. She says that, for her, it made it 'almost worth all the trouble' that characterised much of the rest of her time spent at UFS.

Leeds changed her plans and cut short her stay by several months, both because of the tensions she experienced over race and other identity markers, and because of concerns about a lack of academic rigour and resources at UFS.

Jansen traces some of the hate talk that Leeds heard in Bloemfontein to fear. He's seen that fear in the faces of white South Africans in a class he teaches for first-year students. The topic is how to deal with a shared, violent past. Jansen tells me:

It's very uncomfortable for the students, the white students especially. Any talk of the past gets them so uptight. No matter how you present it, no matter how empathetically. No matter the fact that you talk about the Boer War, not apartheid only. They get so uptight.

And it's because of all the other things happening around them. The sense that affirmative action has taken away their place in the sun. The fact that they feel they're being attacked by political voices all the time. The fact that they have heard their fathers talk about land being taken away without compensation. There's a vulnerability that becomes particularly acute when the past gets mentioned. They think it's accusatory.

The reaction is nuanced. Some students, black and white, do enjoy the 'difficult grappling with the past' that Jansen encourages. And when those who are less comfortable ask him why he insists on the conversation, he has a carefully thought-out answer: 'We talk about the past always being present. I give four or five examples of how, even though we tried to get out of the past, it keeps showing up.' Like the way the Reitz video showed up.

Then, Jansen asks his students: 'Now, don't you think it's a good idea to learn the skills – emotional, psychological, intellectual, spiritual – to be able to deal with the past in such a way that you can imagine a different future?'

Facing and History Ourselves

10. The languages we speak

To imagine a future together, South Africans need a common language. At first glance, that might seem impossible in a nation with 11 official languages. But I find a number of South Africans I meet to be language travellers – their linguistic ability encompasses a number of the official languages. They are able to find ways to share wherever they are, in whatever tongue suits the occasion.

Nthabiseng Khotseng is one of those adept at unpacking the language that suits the moment. She enrolled at UFS when her father, Benito Khotseng, came to work at the university as a pioneering black administrator. I met her in her office in Bloemfontein, where she works as a manager in charge of training for the Free State Provincial Government. I'm curious about her experiences as part of the first sizeable wave of black students who went to the university in the 1990s.

She tells me how she might not have gone to UFS had the choice been entirely her own. She spoke Sotho at home and had attended integrated junior and high schools where the teaching medium was English. Now, she was about to go to a predominantly Afrikaans university, and she was apprehensive. The tuition fees were waived because her father worked at UFS and she also saw an opportunity to help her father build a new character for the university. Khotseng lived with her family off campus, so she escaped some of the worst racial clashes in and around the residences. She enrolled as an undergraduate for the university's well-regarded occupational-therapy degree, where classes were taught in the medical school, set slightly apart from the rest of the campus, which had a buffering effect.

'You were kept away a lot from what was happening in the hostels,' she says. 'But you could obviously sense the tension on campus. There were times when we felt very, very unsafe. It was still during a difficult time in our country.'

When she was at the university, Khotseng's teachers and fellow students called her by her Sotho name, Nthabiseng, which means 'makes me happy'. This is significant in a country where black South Africans were once routinely expected to change their names when they entered white-run institutions like schools and churches, or went to work in the homes, offices and factories owned by white South Africans. Sotho and Zulu and Xhosa names were hard to pronounce, English and Afrikaner South Africans complained. The indigenous names were also unwelcome because they were pre-Western and pre-Christian. That's why the world came to know the man as Nelson Mandela, although as a little boy he was Rolihlahla, Xhosa for 'pulling the branch of a tree' or 'troublemaker'.

'Africans of my generation – and even today – generally have both a Western and an African name,' Nelson Mandela writes in his autobiography. 'Whites were either unable or unwilling to pronounce an African name, and considered it uncivilised to have one. That day, Miss Mdingane [Mandela's first teacher] told me that my new name was Nelson. Why she bestowed this particular name upon me I have no idea.'[51]

Khotseng tells me a story that both is and is not about race in 21st-century South Africa. A few weeks before we met, she had been called into school for a meeting with her nine-year-old son's principal and teacher because her child had had a fight with a white classmate. Khotseng found that the teacher, the principal and the other child's parents were concerned that race may have been at the heart of the fracas in their middle-class, once all-white, school.

'Let's look at what was the core problem,' she told them at the meeting. The children had claimed the same toy, and 'that boy, whether he was black or white, had hit my son with a stone and hadn't apologised.

'It was over a ball. It was over a ball. It was over a *ball*,' Khotseng says, and with each repetition of the sentence she sounds more incredulous that the other adults had missed that point.

'I'm not so quick to pull the colour card, but sometimes you realise other people are more focused on the colour card,' she says.

Looking back on her years at UFS, Khotseng says that at times she gave in to pressure to 'be a black person for everyone else. You're so busy fighting, wanting to be in control.'

However, among her fellow occupational-therapy students, a group of 30 in which she was the only black person, race was rarely raised. The white students she knew were academic achievers, too focused on their studies to be able to give much thought to race and politics. Her academic pressure was intense. She was the first black student in the country to earn an occupational-therapy degree – something her father still speaks of with pride.

'You carry this immense responsibility. You don't want to be the one that's first, and fail,' she says. 'Sometimes, I'm amazed at how I did it. I did it in the four years, in the normal time, just like everybody else. I was focused: this is what I want to do; this is what I want to achieve. And I did it.'

Khotseng was taught in Afrikaans at university. The textbooks, at least, were in English. And she was allowed to answer exam questions in English. Although the university had determinedly built an Afrikaans classroom culture, it's not uncommon, even today, to find lecturers teaching in Afrikaans but assigning English textbooks, particularly in the sciences.

'You miss the context of the teacher explaining. That whole engagement with the teacher, you miss out,' Khotseng says. At times, during classes, she had to ask a fellow student to translate.

Khotseng succeeded studying in Afrikaans, and believes the experience has helped broaden her understanding of herself and her country. She feels that Afrikaner students studying in English might find the same. What are her thoughts on Afrikaner students who today still cling to Afrikaans? She feels it's a shame: 'I think a lot of white students are clinging to what they think is a reality they've lost. They're not willing to embrace where we are now. And that's sad.'

She advises black students at the university today, however, not to rise to every challenge, every racist or racial comment. 'Choose your battles, when you have to be firm and assertive,' she says. 'Balance what you can win, what you can gain. The younger you are, the more emotional you are. You've got to bring balance.'

She also has advice for today's white UFS students:

Open your eyes. Be more human. Be more understanding. Have a lot more empathy for black people, who really are disadvantaged in ways you don't understand. Take the opportunity of discovering people who are different from you. Be more open to experiencing life in a different way. Those white students who don't want to embrace change miss out on wonderful people that can make an immense difference in their lives.

The older I've become, the more I've become enlightened, the more I've let up on a lot of issues and a lot of baggage,' she says. 'You begin to realise that friendships and people are beyond colour. Whether or not I like someone has nothing to do with their colour. And I think that's really where the beauty of education comes in: people can learn not to see colour.

Nthabiseng worked for 13 years as an occupational therapist. Now she's a top bureaucrat, a researcher monitoring and evaluating staff training programmes for the Free State provincial premier. And she is a mother. But she finds time to spend weekends tutoring township students, and puts some of her therapy training to use helping young people cope with stress.

In addition to gaining skills, she also believes her work ethic and her character were strengthened during her years at UFS. And, she adds with a laugh, 'people are always so impressed that I speak Afrikaans so fluently'.

Until as recently as 1989, university officials were still insisting Afrikaans would remain the institution's only language of instruction. Yet in that same year, politicians, black and white, were making strides towards reconciliation, which would culminate in the all-race elections of 1994.

With that historic vote, many Afrikaners felt they were set to lose so much – prominence in politics, the assurance of government jobs, business opportunities, power to write their own history, certainty about their future. Everything they thought was permanent was slipping away. What young Afrikaners had assumed from what they had learnt from previous generations to be their God-given rights were now seen by the world as privileges that they had wrested from others.

In 1948 there had been a sense of victory when English was phased out as the language of instruction at UFS. In the 1990s, when English was reintroduced, the spirit was grudging.

'If the Afrikaners try to keep it all, they will lose it all,' argued professors at the time, calling for classes in English and Afrikaans.[52]

The university's official history goes on to spell out the delicate steps then taken, with the focus first on black students enrolled in a university programme called NEED – Need for

Education, Elevation and Development – designed in part to prepare graduates of South Africa's inferior black education system for study at universities formerly reserved for whites.

'On 22 March 1993, in a carefully worded decision, the University Council approved English instruction for students in the NEED programme, as well as gradual implementation of a parallel-medium programme of instruction for "other students who have problems with Afrikaans".'[53]

As more and more black students – referred to in the university history as 'students who have problems with Afrikaans' – enrolled, more and more English courses were offered. This was happening against a broader context across South Africa, in which white South Africans were accused of using language to justify barring black South Africans not just from universities, but also from junior and high schools. When white South Africans talked of wanting to preserve and protect their culture, black South Africans heard it as a stubborn, racist attempt to justify preserving the privileges apartheid had created for the country's minority.

Billyboy Ramahlele said that when he first came to the university in 1996, the 'dominant culture was an Afrikaans culture. Whatever that means. Culture, in South Africa, is race. If you say culture, you are saying black or white.'

A new South Africa, some of its black and white citizens dared to imagine, would be a nation in which cultures and traditions worth preserving would be shared. Being multilingual would identify a South African as much as his or her passport.

In 2003 a new policy was adopted by the university that embraced both English and Afrikaans as the university's main languages, and that pledged to help develop the use of Sotho on campus. Today, at the entrance to the university, visitors are greeted by three concrete plinths engraved with the words 'Universiteit van die Vrystaat'; 'University of the Free State'; 'Yunivesithi Ya Freistata'. Every course is offered in Afrikaans and English. Afrikaners can isolate themselves in Afrikaans classes, while the English classes are predominantly filled by black South Africans from many ethnic backgrounds, and some English-speaking white South Africans who have ventured to the Free State.

In 2005, two years after the multilingual policy was adopted, the university administration renewed its efforts at integration, noting in an annual university review the separation of classes and continuing segregation in the halls of residence. The challenge, university officials wrote in their review, was 'creating a sense of belonging for all. It is about black and white taking non-racialism seriously, literally unlearning old habits of racism, discrimination and racial thinking patterns.'[54]

In his inaugural address in 2009 as the university's first black rector, Jansen touched on a wide range of issues. The *Sunday Times*, drawing attention to a paragraph many South Africans would read with interest, reprinted the speech in full under the headline 'Afrikaans here to stay'.[55] Jansen said in the speech:

I am deeply committed to the promotion of Afrikaans and Sesotho at the University of the Free State. Many of you have asked me to do away with Afrikaans in the name of pragmatism. Let me be clear: that will not happen on my watch. We will respect the history of this institution and its founding language. Rather than do away with languages, we should embrace more languages. I will in 2010 open discussion on ways in which we can get every white student to learn Sesotho or Setswana and every black student to learn Afrikaans, and all our students to learn to write and speak English competently.[56]

Three years later, Jansen was still resisting the call from some black students to drop Afrikaans. He tells me he urges them to 'understand the history of the country', understand that Afrikaners see the marginalisation of their language as a step towards 'blotting them out' as a people.

Under apartheid, black students were forced to learn Afrikaans, which they saw as the language of the white oppressor. The 1976 student riots in Soweto were sparked in part by rage against instruction in Afrikaans.

Jansen wants an integrated campus, and he fears Afrikaner flight. He senses the university is near a tipping point, he says. Of the once all-white university's 30 000 students who were registered in 2012, 60 per cent were black. South Africa's total population of 50 million is 80 per cent black. The Free State's population, among South Africa's least-populated provinces, of about 2,7 million, is more than 80 per cent black.

Jansen tells black students to be more tolerant and generous. He wants them to see that forgiveness and generosity are not just personal choices, but a duty of leaders in a fledgling democracy. He notices a political agenda – targeting the speakers and not the language – in some of the arguments against Afrikaans.

The conventional wisdom – the stereotype, if you will – is that white South Africans hold the advantage in any encounter with black South Africans. Jansen is turning that on its head, and forcing all students to contemplate what that requires of them. Will black students try to take advantage and amass more privileges, as some white South Africans did during the apartheid years, or will they take on the challenges of ensuring no one abuses power in the future? Will white students retreat into victimhood, demanding protection, or step into a broader world, with all the challenges that entails?

Jansen also points out that Afrikaans is not just the home language of some white South Africans, but of the coloured community too, which traces a strain of its ancestry to the first people of southern Africa, the Khoisan.

'Understand that for a lot of people who were here first, by the way, the use of Afrikaans has a rich historical and social and cultural meaning,' he tells students. 'Simply blotting it out would not just alienate a lot of Afrikaans people, it would destroy our attempts to build an integrated campus.'

Some black students ask why, since they are struggling in English, usually their second language, white students should have the advantage of studying in their mother tongue. But

Jansen is suspicious of that logic. The notion that someone is 'giving up their mother tongue is simply disingenuous,' Jansen says, arguing that many black South Africans, from early in their school days, surrendered Zulu, Sotho, Xhosa, or other languages spoken at home, in favour of English in the classroom.

'It's not the best English. And it's probably not the best thing pedagogically,' Jansen explains, but goes on to say that black students' use of English often start long before they come to UFS, while many Afrikaans-speakers at UFS come from rural areas, where their exposure to English is minimal and their entire schooling regularly takes place in Afrikaans. Black South Africans may indeed be more at home in a multilingual world.

While Jansen is calling for tolerance on the language question, he also believes it will ultimately be resolved in favour of English, as a matter of practicality. When he makes that prediction, he may have in mind students like Magon Mouton, who grew up speaking Afrikaans in her mixed-race community in the Northern Cape.

Mouton could take classes in her theatre and psychology majors in Afrikaans, but she has chosen to study in English. That's the best way to prepare, she believes, for the possibility of one day studying or working overseas. 'But I'm still Afrikaans at heart,' she says. 'As long as people still speak in Afrikaans and sing in Afrikaans and think in Afrikaans, it's going to survive.'

Afrikaner students and lecturers have different reactions to the language question. Ladine van der Walt, a medical student from Pretoria, considers the question during a conversation in a sunny residence courtyard with a fellow medical student and participant in the F1 programme, Bernhard Louw. Their classes in Afrikaans, they say, are white classes.

For Van der Walt, it should be a matter of fairness. At the university, speakers of South Africa's 10 other official languages share English classes, while Afrikaners hold onto Afrikaans, she says. 'I think it's really selfish.'

Louw thinks differently: 'I want education in my own language,' he declares, saying he was raised to feel protective of Afrikaans, though he acknowledges that means he will have few students from other cultures and races in his classes. Louw acknowledges that Afrikaners may one day have to yield on the language issue. But he feels that the change must be eased in, starting with schools, and not be left until university. He presents it as a practical strategy. Others may hear it as a stalling tactic.

I also visited Annette de Wet, who came to the university first as a postgraduate student of Afrikaans. Now she teaches Afrikaans and linguistics. She coordinates a literacy programme at a centre devoted to improving students' skills at UFS.

De Wet was nervous at being asked to do an interview in English. She prepared a two-page document laying out her feelings about change at UFS and across South Africa. The document was testament to the importance she places on communicating. She may feel vulnerable as a minority in a changing country, but engages with the issue bravely. In her courage and optimism, perhaps she is not in the minority. Race and language don't tell her whole story.

'I think I can express myself very well in Afrikaans. I sound a little bit dumb to myself when I speak in English,' she says, before belying that during a fluent, and often quietly passionate, conversation.

As a student, De Wet had tackled the question of whether Afrikaans was a fully-fledged language. She concluded it has the simplified grammar and tendency to borrow from other cultures that characterise a Creole dialect. But she also concluded that Afrikaners had raised it to a language in its own right, with an extensive literature and vocabulary developed for the courts and higher education.

'We are quite proud of what Afrikaans has achieved,' she says. 'We're just, almost, sad at having to lose all that.'

De Wet, as carefully elegant in her dress as in her language, reflects on the future of Afrikaans as an academic language when English is a global language. Scholars can gain international exposure when they publish in English, and that is not just true of Afrikaans scholars, but of scholars around the world for whom English is not a home language. Afrikaans is a strong language, and books and music in Afrikaans are flourishing at the moment, she says, while contemplating the possibility it could one day be relegated to a 'conversational' language. English, meanwhile, would come into its own as the language that can unify South Africa and link its people to the rest of the world.

'This is actually part of being in the global village. I actually think more and more languages are going to go this way.'

She knows such predictions can leave fellow Afrikaners fearful and angry. She is philosophical as she reflects on the radical changes her university has undergone in a few years:

> Our students and staff compilation are much different from what they were, in that it is not an Afrikaans and white university any more.
>
> Today, something else is more important and that is embracing the variety that our country offers. Either you have your fears of losing something, or you have the excitement of experiencing something new or something better. You have to decide what you want.
>
> I think it's more important to be part of life here. If you want people to honour what's dear to you, you have to honour what's dear to someone else.

Then she surprises me with what at first seems a non sequitur: 'Do you know Orania?' she asks. 'I don't want to live like that. I don't want to be on an island.'

De Wet taught her first linguistics class in English in 2000. She found it changed her thinking about teaching. In Afrikaans, she was the authority. In English, she sometimes had to ask a student for help finding the right word. 'You almost have to share that [authority]. And I think that's a good thing,' she says, 'because students know they have something to contribute to the teaching situation.'

De Wet searches for the English equivalent of the Afrikaans word '*bevrydend*' to describe the spirit of the time on the UFS campus. She gets up from her desk and reaches for a dictionary, but the English comes to her before she picks it up: 'It's liberating.'

'A campus is a place where you're always going to learn something new. You're always looking for better understanding in your subject, but also in society in the current times. It fits what an academic is there for.'

Working at a university in the midst of change has transformed her.

'I think I've grown as a person. I've grown as an academic.'

11. Choosing to lead

Vincent Khetha's memories of his early days at UFS are of violence, rejection, insults – and worse. A couple of decades later, Khetha, who was in the first wave of the black-student intake at UFS, has transformed his past into lessons that guide him every day in his work as a government department manager, by making the same kind of choice his alma mater has put before the current students.

It is, in a way, a choice that we all have to make. The choice that can make a leader.

More astonishing to me, Khetha has also made the choice to return to UFS, as a student and as a mentor to other students. He also plans for his own children to study at the university. He could certainly not have imagined that happening when he first enrolled as a social-science student at his hometown university in 1995, when he was 25.

Back then, Khetha knew the university had a reputation for being hostile to black students. He had the grades to get into the prestigious University of the Witwatersrand, but his family did not have the money to send him there.

Khetha's mother worked as a cashier at UFS, which meant her children were entitled to six years' free education there. His parents scraped together money for the extra cost of housing him on campus, allowing a little more space for his brother and sister in the family's tiny home.

Khetha remembers being told that the swimming pool at the residence to which he had been assigned was for whites only. His res was supposedly integrated when he arrived, but he says that white students there were pressurised by white students from other hostels to join them. The white students at his residence decided to move out, one by one.

His original res was then turned into offices for the university's medical staff, and he was moved to another res, Olienhout. Again, he witnessed white flight. Soon he was living in an all-black res with neighbouring all-white reses. The white neighbours would hurl racial epithets and stones at Khetha and his housemates as they walked to and from classes. The white students declared the pavement was for the use of whites only.

On one occasion, white students threw smoke bombs into Khetha's campus home. A friend was badly injured jumping from a window to escape the acrid fumes, Khetha says. The friend's teeth were smashed. Black students responded by breaking the windows of white students' cars. Many of the whites from Khetha's residence had moved into Reitz. It seemed to Khetha the university was transferring the problem to Reitz.

Khetha contends that the white students should have instead been told that, if they did not want to integrate, they should leave the university. Later, Reitz became infamous for the racist video. It might yet be remembered as the spark that set off a cleansing conflagration – the crisis that forced real change.

Khetha and his housemates, meanwhile, made some changes at their residence. He became its 'prime,' the head of a student management committee. This committee devised a new motto, new colours and a new name for the residence. It was christened Khayalami, meaning 'our home' in Zulu. It was the first res at UFS with an African name. Unwelcome as they felt on campus, Khetha says, he and his colleagues had made a firm decision: 'We've got to stay here. We need to organise ourselves.'

Kyalami (same sound, different spelling) is a motor-racing circuit in Johannesburg. Khetha explains that some white students believed there was a cool connection with racing, and applied to live in Khayalami. Once they arrived on campus, senior white students persuaded them to leave for white residences.

By then English had been adopted as a second official language of instruction at UFS to accommodate the learning requirements of black students. However, Khetha says it wasn't unusual to turn up for a class scheduled to be taught in English to discover a professor insisting on teaching in Afrikaans. Lecturers complained that they had taught in their mother tongue all their careers and could not be expected to change overnight. One told his class, 'You must tell whoever is talking about integration to appoint English lecturers.'

Khetha believes that for all the sincerity behind senior university officials' talk of integration, they had no real idea how to go about it. They had no system to monitor whether their policies on integrating the residences and teaching in English were in reality carried out. White students and white teachers read a message in the absence of such oversight: that for all their talk, the top university administration lacked real commitment to change.

Khetha was also aware that outside the university certain parties were agitating. Conservative white politicians opposed integration at UFS. Khetha saw an email sent to university staff by a political party calling for protest marches to oppose the changes the administration was demanding.

Khetha joined a university transformation committee. He was convinced that, by allowing racism and segregation to be perpetuated, university officials were failing black and white students alike. He says he told his fellow committee members that the university was 'a good platform to prepare students for the corporate world. There won't be any boardroom for whites, a boardroom for blacks: it will be one company. We're not preparing students for this. In fact, we're confusing them.'

As he neared the completion of his bachelor's degree in social science, Khetha began to feel the university was finally making progress. The heads of the residences were told that if they did not support integration, they would have to leave, he says.

Khetha now manages a provincial-government arts and culture programme that oversees museums and designs projects to teach South Africans about their national symbols, including the new anthem adopted after apartheid.

As a bureaucrat, Khetha says he has been able to put into practice the lessons he learnt the hard way at university. When he sees his staff separating into black and white camps, he takes people aside and tells them he wants to see black and white employees working together. He is able to share his personal history, and tells his team that segregation 'did not work at my university, and it cannot work here. We don't have two goals, to say we want white officials to achieve one goal and we want black officials to achieve another goal. It's one goal,' he says.

He says he used to view Afrikaans as the language of the enemy when he was younger, and regrets he didn't take advantage of his days at UFS to become more fluent in the language. 'I think Afrikaans is a very important language,' he says. 'To have learnt it would have benefited me.'

Khetha's a frequent visitor to his old res, Khayalami, which remains predominantly black. There, he urges students to get to know their white counterparts. He also counsels them not to expect to get ahead on the colour of their skin. Affirmative action, he tells them, should and will fade away as the country moves toward Mandela's dream of a society where race does not matter.

'One day, it's going to expire,' he says of affirmative action. 'There's no better life for people who are lazy. Those are the things that we should talk about. Even at work.'

He doesn't just visit his alma mater to give motivational talks. Since completing his first degree at UFS, he has gone back to study for degrees in cultural anthropology, history, public administration and political science. Now he's working on a master's in environmental management.

If he fails an exam now, he says, he knows it's because he didn't do enough work. In the old days, he would worry that poor grades reflected a racist professor's preconceptions, or perhaps his own difficulty following lectures in Afrikaans.

In a decade, when his eldest child will be ready for university, he expects her to go to UFS. By then everything will be in place, he says. 'We will have achieved real transformation. Development is a process. The biggest mistake is that we want things to be done now.'

To revolt against change is futile. To embrace it, as Khetha did, is to find that the story does not end. Moving towards change is a choice that brings not resolution, but the exhilaration of more choices, more opportunities to lead or be led.

Take, for instance, Eddie de Wet. He could have chosen a tradition-bound residence at UFS and become a leader in a generations-old mould among other Afrikaners. Instead, he has reached out to other South Africans who come from many traditions, and established himself as a new kind of leader. De Wet, still studying at UFS as I write this, could have set out on a patriarchal path but instead he has chosen to honour his mother and the choices she did not have.

Lizelle Oosthuizen wisely told her son that the opportunity he received of attending the study programme in the US came with certain responsibilities. Some of the South Africans who made that trip acknowledge they were at first drawn simply by the chance of a free ticket abroad. What adventurous young adult wouldn't be? They applied, wrote essays, attended interviews.

They were accepted and flown halfway around the world. And since that flight, they have been faced with the choice of embarking on unexpected, sometimes tumultuous, inner journeys. Although most sensed that more than a free jaunt was on offer when they first saw the posters urging them to apply for F1, they could only have had an inkling then of what they would shoulder. And they may not even fully understand the responsibility until they are older and come to look back on their personal histories, which are bright threads in a stirring tapestry. Did they change the future? That task, which stands before us all, will never be complete.

Khetha is a study in optimism, a man able to look ahead after having gone through some of the most difficult years at UFS. Today's students are part of a more considered, more assured project. And, unlike Khetha's generation, they did not grow up knowing apartheid.

Not that you can erase history with a free trip overseas. Who would want to? Without our pasts, how would we ever learn about second chances?

F1 participant Magon Mouton once told me that in her home town, Upington, it's still normal to walk into a restaurant and find white people in one section, blacks in another and coloureds in another. There are no laws mandating this casual segregation – it's just that people don't question it.

Mouton was once among them, she says, describing how, almost unconsciously, she used to scan the racial pattern of a dining room and go immediately to the table closest to the

blacks or coloureds. Now, she makes an effort to cross that in-
visible line and take a table in the 'white section'.

'I'm trying to embrace change,' she says. 'I kind of opt for a
different table.'

Her friends and her mother view her new boldness in restaurants as one of the ways in which she has changed since
going to the US. Friends also notice that she now enjoys traditionally black African food like stew with pap, which her friends
say they hate, and that she listens to Afrikaans pop music. They
don't quite know what to make of her. Some say, 'You're so
white now'; others say, 'You're so black now.'

Mouton says she has simply matured. 'I can make my own traditions. I can make my own values.'

It's almost too perfect. But it's true.

12. The human project

A young Afrikaner woman studying today at UFS makes me think of Frederick Fourie in his early days as rector about a decade ago. She is among the students I interviewed over the course of several visits I made to Bloemfontein.

The woman, who went to Texas as an FI envoy, launched on her return an elegant, weaponless guerrilla war. Her tactics include sitting in a different seat every time she goes to class. At every res meeting, she talks to someone with whom she might not normally have engaged. Although Afrikaans is her mother tongue, she stubbornly raises questions in English during the res meetings. She knows her Afrikaans friends expect her to speak in Afrikaans, but also knows that Afrikaans leaves most of the black students feeling excluded.

I suspect that among both the black and white students she encounters are those who are put off balance without quite knowing why. Likewise, some of Fourie's colleagues, both black and white, probably did not quite know what to make of him. And some might have been inspired to seek their own self-transformation.

As a young student in the 1970s, Fourie had encountered a professor who had studied abroad. That planted an ambition. Fourie, who had lost both his parents by the time he started university, went on to study for his doctorate at Harvard after completing bachelor's and master's degrees at UFS. Now, Fourie applauds Jansen, the rector who took on the task of accelerating transformation at the university, for sending young students abroad as part of their education. 'You are sowing seeds. That's what education is,' Fourie says. Nevertheless, he has concerns:

> I am acutely aware of the huge challenges deriving from the multilayered and multifaceted nature of institutional culture. For example, I think such student leadership development is a brilliant idea. But I suppose I have the question: 'How deep and lasting is the impact on the university as an organisation?'
>
> There are so many challenges. How do you change institutions, the 'deep' institutional culture of a place? Where do you put energy? Where does your transformation energy go? I have no obvious answer for that, for striking the balance between, for example, student leadership and other dimensions of the university.

He goes on to list those dimensions – in no particular order – from attitudes of staff, parents and alumni who may oppose against change, to issues that go beyond race, including sexism.

Some might argue that expending energy and resources for change on student leaders (and Jansen is grooming those chosen for the F1 programme to be leaders) – a number of whom leave every year – will have limited impact. And those few hundred student leaders who get a chance to travel abroad for the programme are only a small percentage of the student body.

Furthermore, at UFS one only need look at the persistence of traditions at the residences, controlled by generation after generation of students, despite efforts by generation after generation of university administrators to influence them. Now, however, Jansen is hoping a new group of young people will create a new culture that will persist.

Students come to UFS from the schools, communities and churches that produced their elders, bringing with them attitudes that have developed over generations. But change is possible, if, sometimes, at the pace of one conversation at a time.

Fourie found his time in the US 'life-changing. Spending time overseas changes your horizons.'

After completing his doctorate at Harvard, Fourie chose to return to teach at UFS. He was seen as something of a rebel on the tradition-bound campus, and when his university found itself confronted with change, it turned to Fourie, making him rector in 2003. Fourie resigned in 2008, exhausted after the Reitz video emerged, which underlined the depth of opposition he faced among white students, as well as white parents, alumni, staff and even university managers.

Yet today Fourie is still involved with the economics faculty, and is very attached to his university. 'I'm a very loyal person,' Fourie says. 'If I work somewhere, I'm there to build it.'

A few years ago, Fourie ran into a friend from his Harvard days who had gone on to work at the International Monetary Fund. The friend complained that his influence over policy was minimal. Fourie knows he could have followed a career path similar to his friend's. He is glad he chose instead to come home:

> In this country, you're closer to change. We are still shaping the fundamentals of a new society. One can have an impact. That is why I did not stay to pursue a career and life in the US. South Africa, and Bloemfontein and UFS, is my place.
>
> That's why I'm still here.

Jansen has seen the strides that the students who have taken part in the F1 programme can make, and wants to ensure they have the support to continue to grow once they are back home. He sees the students in F1 becoming increasingly prominent as those we might call the students of the Reitz era – the temporal and moral place in which the racist video was made – have now left UFS.

'I saw the returnees take over a university event, and talk assertively about the future. They would actually testify . . . to the other students,' Jansen tells me. (He means they testify in the sense of an evangelical believer attempting to make converts.) He says that F1 students have become the political and intellectual centre of the campus:

> And as the older students left or graduated, those are the guys who had the memory of Reitz, the better it became. We generated the next year's leadership, the student leadership, from the group. So you would see increasingly, as we're moving into the second

and third year [of F1], the student leaders across the board, of all the associations, would have included F1 students.

It was a combination of the old guys moving out and the ones we had invested in heavily through F1 and other things beginning to take centre stage. Because they had no direct memory of Reitz. And then they became very prominent in the residences.

And residences are the heart of student life at UFS, repositories of generations of ritual and shapers of new traditions.

'So the residence leadership had these kids who had lived in residences in other countries,' Jansen continues. 'And they came back and said, "We can do this differently. We can add value to this."'

The F1 students also had an impact in the classrooms, which, at UFS, are as tradition-bound as the residence halls. 'They would complain about their professors,' Jansen explains. 'They said, "You know, we were just at Cornell, or wherever, and the students would actually ask questions."'

So, in all these ways, says Jansen, this new generation of students infused throughout the university a sense of diligence, optimism and change. And a sense of expectation: 'We can actually get better lecturers. We can actually get better services,' he says.

There was resistance, nevertheless, from both university staff and other students. 'A number of faculty members, particularly the people who've never themselves had international experience, see this as being uppity,' Jansen says.

He thinks that some of them can be quite unkind. They have the attitude, 'You see what happens when there's a rector who studied in the US and then takes the kids to the US? They come back with all these foreign ideas.' They never voice their concerns to Jansen directly, but he senses the resistance.

He also picked up differences between the returnees, as he calls the students who have been abroad, and the larger student community, at an age when people often simply want to blend in. He says the F1 students discuss subjects like race and history, which their peers prefer to avoid. Even their hopefulness can seem like an unwelcome challenge to those, white and black, who believe South Africa cannot hope to change. 'In a crowd, I could pick out the F1 students,' Jansen says. 'They would talk differently. They would hope differently,' he says.

Jansen is concerned that the F1 participants will stand out so much from their fellow students that they will end up feeling isolated. He also worries that they will spend so much time working on their F1 projects that they won't devote enough time to their studies.

Those who have participated in the programme can seem torn. Do their old friends think they are pretentious? Are they doing enough? Are they doing so much they are neglecting their personal ambitions? After all, this is an ambitious group of would-be professionals.

For the black students, it's the 'acting white' label that stings, as well as accusations they are letting themselves be fooled or used by whites who are insincere about nonracialism; and the white students can be accused of betraying their own tightly knit community.

Manto Rantsho, an accounting student from Welkom, says her parents fear she will one day be rebuffed or hurt by the white friends who are part of her F1 group which went to Texas. She says she understands her parents' perspective, honed by decades of apartheid. Younger black South Africans have also inherited that fear, she says, describing how some of her fellow black students struggle to understand why she has taken up Jansen's transformation challenge. They tell her she's wasting her time; the leopard never changes its spots.

She says older black students tell her she should follow their lead: concentrate on her studies and graduate on to real life as soon as she can. They tell her she can be hopeful, but they are not.

'You wouldn't know because you haven't gone through what's been happening,' they tell her. 'They still have a lot of questions and anger,' Rantsho says.

Rantsho roomed with a white American student during her time in Texas. 'I'd never shared a house with a white person. I was way out of my comfort zone.'

In the end, though, she came to think of her room-mate as her friend, not a white person. She realised change can be possible, if not easy. She imagines her parents would be tense if she were to bring a white friend home to Welkom for the weekend. But she believes they would accept it, and perhaps begin to ask themselves, 'Why do we have so much hatred?'

At a meeting with students who had recently returned from abroad, the dean of student affairs at UFS set them to work, dividing them into small groups to talk about what they had seen and heard while overseas. What did foreign universities have that their university needed? When the students had completed their brainstorming, several themes emerged, each written up on large sheets of paper taped to the walls of a residence common room.

In the urban campus of Cleveland State University, the library stays open through the night, points out a student who had recently returned from the American Rust Belt. The South African students, whose own country combines elements of the developing and developed worlds, marvel at the infrastructure of well-endowed universities in developed countries. The South Africans tell of how they had access abroad to free Wi-Fi and how there were ramps and automatic doors that make US campuses user-friendly for students in wheelchairs. There were buses that make sprawling campuses accessible to students without cars. The car is a symbol of post-apartheid South Africa's racial wealth gap. When black South Africans reach middle-class status, they often mark the achievement with the purchase of a flashy car.

As well as bricks and mortar and motors, the South Africans saw that foreign universities had built a sense of community. Students thought of themselves as Texas Aggies and Cornell Bears, not just members of a res.

Overseas, the South Africans observed that the students questioned their professors, and their teachers responded to them as equals. At UFS, they complain, professors too often want rote answers to their own questions, and treat queries from students as challenges. Overseas, the students 'control the lecture, because they're independent thinkers,' a South African student points out.

And independent actors. The students they met abroad, others added, were engaged in all manner of social issues, and did not wait for professors or administrators to lead them. The South Africans sat in on the clubs of lesbian and gay groups in Europe, and of environmentalists in the US. Diversity wasn't just about black and white race groups, but also about understanding the role of, for example, Mexican immigrants and their descendants in the US, or feeding the hungry on an economically diverse campus, or tackling the impact of global warming.

The South Africans saw that students their age in other countries were confident they could change the world. However, they also saw that other countries too have unresolved problems and they gained confidence from observing that some foreigners look to South Africans for solutions.

Despite his natural reserve, Nyakallo Scheepers gave his views during a social-justice class in Texas when the subject of affirmative action came up. In the US, affirmative action refers to attempts to ensure that black people who have experienced discrimination as a class have opportunities in the workplace. In South Africa, similar arguments were made to promote Afrikaner interests in the 1950s, and, since 1994, the interests of blacks and others, including women. Scheepers said that in his Texas class, some people were saying, no, this thing is unfair. Others were saying it restores equity. I said to them that when people bring such laws, every single person in a seat of power, when he makes a law, always has some prejudice. I was trying to emphasise that we should look on both sides. Leadership is complex when you're dealing with a nation that's complex. How do you get to that point where you have a leadership that makes decisions that benefit everyone? To get to that is a massive challenge.

Scheepers says that he came to realise in Texas that teaching people about other cultures is one way to meet that challenge: 'The more they get educated, the more they disregard the differences and see people as equal.'

Scheepers says his visit to the US also helped him gain empathy for white South Africans, who are a minority in their homeland, as black Americans are in theirs. Scheepers says he can understand why Afrikaners might view black economic empowerment as payback rather than a means of creating opportunities for those who were long denied them. He can also understand why some might resist being taught in anything other than Afrikaans, saying, with a laugh, that he can imagine the uproar among black students if UFS were to propose an all-Afrikaans curriculum.

Scheepers says that before going to Texas, he didn't even think about people of other races. 'I just thought about myself and my close friends. Going there really helped me to relate to different people and know where they're coming from. It really contributed to being able to put myself in other people's shoes before I judge.'

Imagine such a realisation multiplied by 150 – the number of students who participate in F1 each year.

Rector Jansen is known as 'Prof. Jansen' to the students in the class he teaches on understanding the violence and divisions of South Africa's past. The students bring their parents' fears to the class, he tells me. They have heard during dinner-table conversations of how affirmative action for black South Africans will end opportunities for white South Africans, and of the habit among certain militant black groups of singing apartheid-era protest songs about killing white farmers.

White South Africans have read Afrikaans newspaper stories about black farm workers seizing land from white farmers, and have heard the relentless chorus by Afrikaner media and lobbying groups about crime and corruption, which has clear, if coded, racial overtones.

'There's a vulnerability,' Jansen says. 'Any talk about the past gets them so uptight. The mere fact that we're talking history is enough to drive some kids over the edge.'

Students say they want to put the past behind them. Jansen counters to the effect that that has been tried, and it failed. 'The past keeps coming up. So let's learn emotional, psychological skills to cope,' he tells me, describing his lectures. 'Some of them catch it. A lot of them don't.'

One text that Jansen sets is a letter that Martin Luther King Jr.

wrote from a jail in Birmingham, Alabama. The son, grandson and great-grandson of the family of preachers had been detained for taking part in a civil-rights march in Birmingham in 1963 – a year before Martin Luther King Jr. won the Nobel Peace Prize and five years before he was assassinated. In his cell, he responded to an open letter in which fellow clergymen had advised him to abandon his campaign of non-violent resistance. He expresses disappointment at the white church leaders, but adds, 'I am thankful to God that some noble souls from the ranks of organised religion have broken loose from the paralysing chains of conformity and joined us as active partners in the struggle for freedom.'[57]

Jansen calls that letter 'a beautiful testament of Martin Luther King's understanding of the white clergy, for example, as brothers as opposed to enemies, and yet having to speak to those issues of togetherness in a very direct way'.

Jansen asks his students to assess the class. Then he comes back to his office in the stately early-20th-century building that is the heart of his campus, and pores over the students' reports on their teacher. Often, he says, white students write that going over the past just leaves them feeling shame and remorse.

The philosophy that Jansen brought when he first came to head up the university was that 'there has to be another way of bringing blacks in other than telling whites how bad they are'. Jansen says he acted quite tough on the students who tested the new rules, but also deployed patience and tolerance 'to create a new sense of what you can do'.

And time, he said, is already working its softening magic. Students who were there when the Reitz video was made are moving on, to be replaced by students Jansen believes are slowly overcoming sensitivities about race.

Benito Khotseng, the first senior black member of staff appointed at UFS, has only praise for Jansen:

> What really ought to have been done is what he is doing. We should try to continue changing. The problem with South Africans is we have been exposed to apartheid. Many of us, still, have the knowledge of apartheid. We need to be exposed to an environment where we can begin to learn to work together. Where we can begin to learn to change. If we are not given an opportunity like that, there you find the situations where people go back to an apartheid mentality. We have to create a new South Africa where all people can be accepted as equals.

Khotseng is also proud of what he did as deputy vice chancellor to Coetzee to build a foundation for Jansen. And he recognises that his experience has changed him.

Transformed him?

'I often ask myself whether I have been. But I think that, personally, my attitude toward other people has changed.'

He says his experiences at UFS have led him to commit himself to the proposition that we 'don't have to correct the old apartheid by discriminating against white people. I believe that has been changed in my heart.'

Because of his time at UFS, Khotseng has also learnt that

many Afrikaners want to break out of the stereotype in which many other South Africans insist on confining them. He has seen something of how Afrikaners can feel hemmed in, unwanted, and of how they can feel that South Africa is, both because of and despite their history, the only place they can call home.

'They feel more left out. So we black people need to be more open,' Khotseng says. 'I think the Afrikaners want to be accepted.'

Khotseng saw it in his colleagues' faces when, armed with his Sotho phrase book, they received warm responses as they greeted campus cleaners and gardeners in their mother tongue.

And he saw it in 2009, after he left the university, when he was travelling to a conference in London. A UFS graduate recognised him at Heathrow. The Afrikaner student was very excited to bump into the ex-professor and told him that he was now working as an occupational therapist at a London hospital, where he found himself held up as an example of how to operate in a multicultural environment. The graduate said he had learnt to reach out to people from all over the world as a student – by listening to Khotseng.

The university renamed a building housing its centre for the development of higher education after Khotseng when he retired in 2003. In 2004, the year it celebrated its centenary, the university awarded him a medal for his 'leadership in transformation'. However, Khotseng knows that change cannot be memorialised. He says the UFS project must be constantly nurtured and trained and expanded, 'if we honestly want to, in the end, win the fight against apartheid'.

Billyboy Ramahlele, who was head of the Kiepersol residence back in the early days of transformation at UFS, says the Reitz video crisis taught him that people can easily slip back into old, dark patterns: 'You just can't leave the situation unattended.'

Ramahlele believes Jansen has made an important contribution by making the 'human project' a priority, by focusing on teaching students about why they need to integrate, on 'educating our students about humanness'.

'We do not just force you to live together for the sake of living together. The world outside is integrated. It's black and white living together, pink and purple people.'

Ramahlele is still at UFS, and is one of its longest-serving black administrators. He now directs programmes that encourage students to take part in community service, such as volunteering to tutor children in impoverished high schools or help doctors and nurses at township clinics.

Ramahlele can remember a time when black students needed special permission from the government to study at the university. His two children, a 12-year-old son and a 14-year-old daughter, were born at the university hospital and grew up in campus accommodation. He also expects them to attend UFS one day:

> This is a good university. I believe in this university. I believe in the quality of its academic offerings. We are a university that is number one, really dealing with South African problems.
>
> After the Reitz video, somebody said to me, 'Are you not

ashamed to be associated with a university of racism?' I told them what's happening here is what's happening in the rest of South Africa. We are a university where Afrikaners and black people meet. They live together. And we are a university working very hard at finding a solution, creating a society where Afrikaners and black people, all of them, can live together. We are a university which is located in a poor province, and our students are poor. Our fee structure responds to this poverty. We are a university that is located in a province where the schooling system is not the best. And, as a university, we are responding to that. We are creating programmes to make sure that even those black students, or students who come from a disadvantaged schooling back-ground, are assisted, are put in programmes that elevate them to the standards of others.

So, we are a university that is taking on South Africa's prob-lems.

As Ramahlele describes it, the challenges ahead now for UFS are at least as great as anything it has faced in its entire history. In his own personal history, he says he survived the night of the Kiepersol siege because he had faith and hope. He still has both.

'I still want to be part of the next change,' he says.

History is not a mere list of facts and dates. It's also about how we tell, and listen to, our common stories – with descriptions, names and labels shifting in unpredictable ways over time.

At Bloemfontein's War Museum of the Boer Republics, erected next to the obelisk raised in honour of the women and children who died in the Anglo-Boer War, curators relate in stark prose the horrific impact the war had on civilians. But the explanatory notes inside the museum use the term 'refugee camps,' not *concentratiekampen* (concentration camps), the term carved in stone on the war memorial.

A museum model the size of a pool table depicts a typical camp, complete with a tiny, poignant cemetery. The curators tell us: 'A shortage of wood or sandstone often resulted in graves being unmarked, or marked by a name in a bottle, placed on a grave.'

Since the end of apartheid, visitors have found accounts of how black South Africans were also caught up in the Anglo-Boer War. The memorial outside is dedicated to the more than 26 000 Afrikaner civilians who died in the camps. Information in the museum adds that 21 000 black South Africans, most of them farm workers and servants, also died in the camps.

A room in the museum has been dedicated to Sol Plaatje, who was born in the Free State in 1876 and who would go on to become a writer, newspaper editor and the first general secretary of the ANC. A sign in the Plaatje Room tells of how 'the black elite who had pinned high hopes on political advancement were deeply disappointed as the peace treaty [that ended the Anglo-Boer War] ensured that the political power would remain in the hands of white South Africans'.

At the entrance to the museum complex, visitors will find the memorial to the Afrikaner civilians who died in war as well as the grave of Emily Hobhouse, the British woman who tried to help them. A sign mounted by the museum makes a proposal: 'When all is said and done, this suffering is not meant to lead to eternal hate and bitterness, but to more profound faith in God, a new future.'

I am reminded of something Coetzee, the former rector, told me during one of our interviews. He related the story of Nelson Mandela's release in 1990 and how he had gathered his three daughters, then children, in front of the family's TV. He told them that they would one day understand they were seeing 'the beginning of a whole new country'.

'But one can never run away from history,' Coetzee cautioned. When he was growing up, he said, his elders would speak about the concentration camps: 'When I was a child, the memories amongst my parents and their friends were still very vivid.'

Coetzee remembers those childhood stories of war and deprivation when he hears white South Africans now complain that black South Africans should stop looking back to apartheid. His relatives could not easily forget their community's darkest days. 'So how can black people easily forget apartheid?' Coetzee asks.

'We need to be very wise – black and white. Things explode so easily with us. We become, so easily, very emotional because the past is not distant. It's only here,' Coetzee said, tapping one hand here, another there, on the tabletop, indicating a mere moment of distance.

'It's not even a generation.'

Epilogue

Whereas some might have heard dissonance, Eddie de Wet heard harmony. It was the 45th anniversary of the founding of De Wet's residence, then named after H. F. Verwoerd, which housed white students only. It is now integrated accommodation and is known as Armentum.

At the reunion, older white men sang the house song they knew from their days as residents there. Their multiracial successors sang a new version of their alma mater, one that has replaced the old residence name with the new.

'Some people sang "Verwoerd" and some people sang "Armentum",' De Wet says. 'They know we actually came from the same place.'

Just before the reunion, as 2013 drew to a close, De Wet's housemates elected him as Armentum's prime, as the head of residence is referred to, for the coming year – a head boy again. De Wet is pleased the former residents still feel they have a place in the house's story – not least because the old residents were as sports-mad as the contemporary ones are (even if rugby is being replaced by soccer as the favourite sport). But, De Wet is more focused on the residence's future. He sees the future in the youngest residents – men he calls 'my first years' in an avuncular tone.

Willy Nel, the professor in charge of mentoring the men of Armentum, has asked the university housing department to direct more non-white students to Armentum. De Wet has embraced the initiative and asked younger members of the house to recruit among black and coloured students.

'We're trying really hard to get the people we feel can belong here and can set the traditions of Armentum, take it forward,' De Wet says.

De Wet has observed the way first years of all races refer to Armentum. As one holiday ended, he noticed how first-year Armentum students updating their social-media accounts said they were 'returning home' to Bloemfontein. 'It's really heartwarming to see the statuses on their way back. That was really something special to me.'

The first years still attend house meetings in suits and ties. Nel had wanted to change that, but tradition doesn't yield easily at UFS. Nel believes dictating what first years wear belittles them; De Wet believes it forges a unity they will need. 'One of my huge goals is to make sure that the first-year group comes in as a unit, to make sure that we have a group taking Armentum into the future.'

South Africans born after apartheid ended aren't free of their nation's history, but they are free, in ways previous generations could not have imagined, to make of it what they will.

The stories I heard on my journeys to the Free State and Texas gave me an understanding of what draws men with vision like

Jonathan Jansen and Alvin Larke to work with young people. I met students in Bloemfontein and College Station who made me wonder what I was doing in my teens and twenties, when I should have been founding my own NGO.

I heard young people trying to find the words to tell the story of a future together, and to tell it to one another. What they talked about made me see possibilities and left me marvelling at the power of even small changes. The way they talked – with humility and without self-regard – made me want to be more open, more self-reflective, more sympathetic.

South African novelist and playwright Zakes Mda says, 'We always sympathise with those whose stories we know.'[58] My grandmother would always save the day's newspaper – significant to me as a news reporter – so she could read it the next morning, in the quiet of her tiny kitchen in a tiny town in Florida. Her example of patience and curiosity – such generous impulses – taught me I could know another's story, even if that someone did not look like me, did not come from my home town or speak my language.

Jonathan Jansen does not look like any of the men who had served before him as head of UFS. But in at least one way he is returning to tradition. Since the 1940s, the vice chancellors at UFS have typically served for a decade or more. Coetzee managed just one five-year term, as did his successor, Fourie. Both served during times of turmoil for the university, and left saying the stress had taken a toll on their health.

Jansen also arrived during a troubled period, but as he embarked on his fifth year he was in a very different place from his predecessors. 'I absolutely enjoy being here,' he tells me. 'I'm completely at ease with the whole of myself.'

He says the campus is different, in subtle but important ways, from what it was like when he arrived:

> Everybody seems to be a bit more relaxed. I see a lot more interracial groups. It's still not ideal, but at least if you think of the almost absolute segregation that one saw in 2009, it's quite heartening to see people just not being scared that they will be categorised or targeted by their own group for any outreach to black or white kids.
>
> I see a peacefulness on campus. Not the almost daily upheavals that we had. People were very angry. It was a whole bunch of issues rolled together, from issues of admissions, of deregistration of students who couldn't pay, to why white students do this and why black students get away with that.

He's even willing to predict that UFS will never again see a race crisis – like the Reitz video affair, which propelled this heartland campus into the centre of an international media storm.

'I sleep comfortably at night, because the hot-button issues, the stuff that was explosive, we've dealt with,' Jansen says.

But he also admits the struggle is far from over – for his university, for Bloemfontein, the city that is its home, and for a country with a troubled past and an uncertain future:

I think in many ways we've gone backward in the broader society. First of all, let's talk about the city. One of the biggest challenges I have today is students who, though they've started to deal with issues of race and ethnicity on the campus, the moment they go to town to the dentist or the gynaecologist or the shop, they run into fairly hard-core racism that hasn't changed. It's either the hard-core black-nationalist politics that can't tolerate white people or the hard-core racism of white folks.

But it's not just Bloemfontein: it happens when they go to Cape Town; it happens when they go to Umtata; it happens when they go to Johannesburg. Those hard-core racial discourses hit them when they hit the country. One of the really problematic stereotypes of South Africa is that Bloemfontein is more racially backward than the rest. That's not my experience as a black person. And that's certainly not my students' experience.

Jansen puts the blame for the racially tense national mood on national leaders, specifically black leaders he believes flame racial tensions with black-nationalist rhetoric. That, he says, makes the project he has undertaken at UFS even more important now than when he first arrived. Jansen says:

What we say to our students is, 'You are not victims. You are in fact the new leadership.' We're training them to go against the grain, and to stand as examples of the tradition of solidarity, the tradition of social justice, the tradition of reconciliation, the tradition of working through difficulties together rather than in conflict.

He is encouraged that many of the students he sent abroad as first years returned to take up student leadership positions. De Wet is not the only one to become a residence prime, and others serve on the student government and help run the student media.

Looking ahead, Jansen says he will continue to focus on students. But he will also devote more time to professors and other staff, offering them guidance in his own very direct way on teaching in a multiracial environment and on the breadth of diversity – racial, ethnic, national, able-bodied versus disabled.

Not that professors are asking to take part in such endeavours. 'Oh no,' Jansen says with a chuckle. 'You're 59 years old. All your degrees come from the same university. You've been teaching in the same way. You don't ask for change. Human beings don't behave that way. We've been having to almost force the issue onto the agenda of the departments of the university.'

He draws strength from the fact that many students have embraced change, though. 'Because they're young. Because they're open-minded. Because they're part of a broader kind of thinking – the Twitter and LinkedIn generation. They know the world is a little bit more interesting than they've been told. And they're idealistic, like young people all over the world.'

As mentioned, pioneering black administrator Benito Khotseng told me of how he was greeted at Heathrow Airport by a former white student of his who had wanted to thank his old prof for helping him learn to live in a diverse world. It strikes me as significant that this encounter happened abroad. Time and again, as I listened to the stories of South Africans, I was struck by how much they had learnt by getting away from home. And listening to them, I also realised how much I've learnt from leaving my own homeland. My travels have led to encounters with grace in unexpected quarters.

And my work on this book has led me to question why, instead of being surprised when humans behave humanely, I don't try more often myself to be fully human. We can all do with being shaken out of our comfort zones from time to time.

Endnotes

1 Pakenham, T. *The Boer War*. Johannesburg and Cape Town: Jonathan Ball Publishers, 2011, p. 331.
2 See http://db.nelsonmandela.org/speeches/pub_view.asp?pg=item&ItemID=-NMS176&txtstr=inauguration (accessed 4 September 2013).
3 Barnard, L. (project leader). *From Grey to Gold: The First 100 Years of the University of the Free State*. Bloemfontein: University of the Free State, 2006, p. 170.
4 Ibid., p. 161.
5 Pakenham, *The Boer War*, pp. 440–441.
6 Ibid., p. 441.
7 Barnard, *From Grey to Gold*, p. 8.
8 Ibid., p. 57.
9 See http://www.sahistory.org.za/people/christiaan-rudolf-de-wet (accessed 19 December 2013).
10 Barnard, *From Grey to Gold*, p. 72.
11 Ibid., p. 71.
12 See http://www.justice.gov.za/trc/special%5Cconscrip/conscr02.htm (accessed 19 December 2013).
13 Barnard, *From Grey to Gold*, p. 55.
14 Ibid., p. 219.
15 Sparks, A. *The Mind of South Africa*. New York: Ballantine Books, 1991, p.192.
16 Ibid., p. 339.
17 Ibid., p. 348.
18 Ibid., p. 337.
19 Crocker, C. *High Noon in Southern Africa: Making Peace in a Rough Neighborhood*. New York: W.W. Norton & Company, 1992.
20 Barnard, *From Grey to Gold*, p. 308.
21 Krog, A. *A Change of Tongue*. Johannesburg: Random House, 2003, p. 167.
22 See http://db.nelsonmandela.org/speeches/pub–view.asp?pg=item&Item-ID=NMS1408&txtstr=NMS1408 (accessed 4 September 2013).

23 See http://www.ufs.ac.za/templates/archive.aspx?news=430&cat=1 (accessed 4 September 2013).

24 See http://www.anc.org.za/docs/jan8/2012/0108.pdf (accessed 4 September 2013).

25 See http://www.anc.org.za/docs/jan8/2012/0108.pdf (accessed 4 September 2013).

26 Bizos, G. *Odyssey to Freedom.* Johannesburg: Random House, 2007, p. 152.

27 Barnard, *From Grey to Gold*, p. 263.

28 Sparks, *The Mind of South Africa*, p. 162.

29 Bizos, *Odyssey to Freedom*, p. 446.

30 Ibid., p. 452.

31 Ibid., p. 453.

32 Mandela, N. *Long Walk to Freedom.* London: Abacus, 1995, p. 438.

33 UFS Planning Unit. *Transformation Plan: 2007–2010.* Bloemfontein: University of the Free State, 2007, p. 9.

34 See http://www.ufs.ac.za/templates/archive.aspx?news=1533&cat=1 (accessed 4 September 2013).

35 See http://www.sahrc.org.za/home/index.php?ipkArticleID=40 (accessed 4 September 2013).

36 See http://www.politicsweb.co.za/politicsweb/view/politicsweb/en/page71619?oid=147446&sn=Detail (accessed 4 September 2013).

37 See http://www.ufs.ac.za/templates/archive.aspx?news=1533&cat=1 (accessed 4 September 2013).

38 Mandela, *Long Walk to Freedom*, p. 462.

39 See http://www.ufs.ac.za/templates/archive.aspx?news=1533&cat=1 (accessed 4 September 2013).

40 See http://www.ufs.ac.za/templates/archive.aspx?news=1533&cat=1 (accessed 4 September 2013).

41 Jansen, J. *Knowledge in the Blood: Confronting Race and the Apartheid Past.* Cape Town: UCT Press, 2009, p. 90.

42 Foote, S. *The Civil War: A Narrative, Volume 2: Fredericksburg to Meridian.* New York: Vintage, 1986, location 3413 of the e-book.

43 Cash, W. *The Mind of the South.* New York: Vintage Books, 1991, p. 173.

44 Dethloff, H. *Texas A&M University: A Pictorial History, 1876–1996.* College Station: Texas A&M University, 1996, location 459 of the e-book.

45 See http://www.pewsocialtrends.org/2012/05/17/explaining-why-minority-births-now-outnumber-white-births/ (accessed 4 September 2013).

46 See http://www.thebatt.com/2.8485/apology-1.1192662#.Uie0VtJwrkc (accessed 4 September 2013).

47 Dethloff, *Texas A&M University*, digital location 869.

48 Brink, A. *A Fork in the Road*. London: Harvill Secker, 2009, pp. 138–139.

49 Ibid., p.141.

50 See http://www.politicsweb.co.za/politicsweb/view/politicsweb/en/page71616/page71656?oid=330512&sn=Detail (accessed 4 September 2013).

51 Mandela, *Long Walk to Freedom*, p. 16.

52 Barnard, *From Grey to Gold*, p. 348.

53 Ibid., p. 348.

54 See http://www.ufs.ac.za/dl/userfiles/Documents/00000/97–eng.pdf (accessed 4 September 2013).

55 See http://www.iol.co.za/news/south-africa/afrikaans-here-to-stay-ufs-principal-1.461792 (accessed 4 September 2013).

56 See http://www.ufs.ac.za/templates/archive.aspx?news=1533&cat=1 (accessed 4 September 2013).

57 King, M. *Letter from the Birmingham Jail*. San Francisco: HarperSanFranciso, 1994, p. 29.

58 Mda, Z. *Sometimes There is a Void: Memoirs of an Outsider*. Johannesburg: Penguin, 2011, p. 156.

List of interviews

Jasmine Bailey, TAMU student
Brooke Brock, TAMU student
Lara Brown, UFS student
Rudi Buys, UFS dean of student affairs
Mikeala Carter, TAMU student
Warren Chalklen, TAMU student
Stef Coetzee, former UFS rector
Mary Conley, College of the Holy Cross professor
Stephanie Curs, TAMU professor
Annette de Wet, UFS professor
Eddie de Wet, UFS student
Frederick Fourie, former UFS rector
Jessica Guerra, TAMU student
Danielle Harris, TAMU vice dean
Chloe Jansen, UFS student
Jonathan Jansen, UFS rector
Vincent Khetha, former UFS student
Benito Khotseng, former UFS deputy vice-rector for student affairs
Nthabiseng Khotseng, former UFS student
Alvin Larke, TAMU professor
Alissa Leeds, Appalachian State University student
Mothusi Lepheane, South African Human Rights Commission
    Free State manager
Bernhard Louw, UFS student
Hugh McElroy, TAMU School of Rural Public Health director of
    institutional advancement
Magon Mouton, UFS student
Susan Mshumpela, former UFS student
Mashudu Ndwammbi, UFS student

Theo Neethling, UFS professor

Willy Nel, UFS professor

Mias Nortier, UFS student

Lizelle Oosthuizen, mother of UFS student

Billyboy Ramahlele, UFS community engagement director

Mano Rantsho, UFS student

James Thomas Reynolds, former TAMU student

Alan Sams, TAMU College of Agriculture and Life Sciences
    executive associate dean

Nyakallo Scheepers, UFS student

Van Aardt Smit, UFS professor

Hussein Solomon, UFS professor

Christine Stanley, TAMU vice president and associate provost for diversity

Martine van der Merwe, UFS student

Ladine van der Walt, UFS student

Karan Watson, TAMU provost and vice president for academic affairs

Donna Whyte, director of Cleveland State University Office of Diversity and
    Multicultural Affairs

Samuel Williams, former TAMU student

Gary Wingenbach, TAMU professor

Acknowledgements

This book was made by many people who gave generously of their time, insight and expertise. Most of their names will be found in the text and in the list of interview subjects. Among others who aided enormously is Lacea Loader, director of strategic communication at UFS, who made introductions, helped me navigate the university's digital archives, and discovered that loaning me a book is a long-term proposition. Catherine Coker and her staff at TAMU's Cushing Memorial Library and Archives facilitated my research there, and responded with memorable calm and competence when an emergency evacuation order interrupted work.

Writing is reading. Undertaking this book meant revisiting the work of authors who have shaped my understanding of South Africa and the US, and discovering work I should have read long ago. I owe a debt to George Bizos, André Brink, W. J. Cash, Alan Cowell, Chester A. Crocker, Henry C. Dethloff, Shelby Foote, Nadine Gordimer, Jonathan Jansen, Martin Luther King, Jr., Antjie Krog, Nelson Mandela, Zakes Mda, Thomas Pakenham, Mamphela Ramphele, Amilcar Shabazz, Elinor Sisulu, Allister Sparks and the UFS team who compiled *From Grey to Gold: The First 100 Years of the University of the Free State* – thanks again, Lacea.

Last, but far from least, my thanks to my commissioning editor, Annie Olivier, and Mark Ronan, the editor.

I hope I have not forgotten anyone. If I have, that error and any others are entirely my own.